In Pursuit of Kate Corbett

by

Anne Loughnane

**Grosvenor House
Publishing Limited**

This book is published by
Grosvenor House Publishing Ltd
28-30 High Street, Guildford, Surrey, GU1 3HY.
www.grosvenorhousepublishing.co.uk

A CIP record for this book
is available from the British Library

ISBN 978-1-907211-57-7

Dedication

In grateful memory of my mother, Margaret Mary Corbett.

Acknowledgements

My thanks are due to the many friends, family members and strangers who helped bring this project to fruition. Foremost amongst these were my four sisters Marie, Kathleen, Mairead and Gemma who helped research the story and provided support and encouragement along the way. The Cistercian nuns of Holy Cross Abbey, Whitland, Wales (formerly of Stapehill Priory, Dorset) and in particular Sister Andrew who offered hospitality and practical help which was much appreciated. Thanks to Norah Quinlevan and Annie Grace of Quin in Co Clare who gave generously of their time and store of anecdotes about the Corbett family. The many friends who provided support and encouragement are too numerous to mention but you know who you are ...thank you. A particular thank you to Moya Cannon, Katherine Dickie, Maureen Kinnell and Catherine Thompson who painstakingly read my early draft and offered helpful feedback.

On the archival front I am indebted to many superb resources such as the National Library Dublin, Clare County Library and Clare Heritage Centre. Wyoming State Archives supplied the photograph used on the back cover and the Charles Belden image used on the front cover was provided by the Charles Belden Collection, American Heritage Centre, University of Wyoming. Particular thanks are due to Roddy Burwell, local Casper genealogist who unearthed so much useful information on the Wyoming front, and a thank you also to Dr. Ciaran O Murchadha who helped with information about local history in Clare. Thank you to family friend

Mary Hannon who provided hospitality and support when I was delving into the records in Clare, and to my cousin Maura Donovan when I was doing so in Dublin. Thanks to Robert McMurray who helped us locate the original site of the homestead and to Tad Knight for bringing us there over the rough track in his pickup truck.

I am indebted to Dorset journalist and author Roger Guttridge for the great photo of the nuns working in the fields. It was taken in 1937 by photographer Harry Ashley working for the Bournemouth Echo and is used on the cover of this book. Thanks to Neal Butterworth, Editor of the Bournemouth Echo who gave me permission to use it. Laura Donnelly, Edinburgh graphic designer, is responsible for the cover design and I am truly grateful for her excellent work, thank you Laura.

Thanks to our three great children, Jamie, Orna and Maeve whose partisan support and loyalty was, as always, a great comfort. Finally and most importantly I need to thank my husband Jim without whose practical and emotional support the project may never have come to fruition. As for so much else in my life I am truly grateful to him.

Contents

FOREWORD

by

Michael Coady

THE UNIVERSE is made up of stories, not atoms – so wrote the American poet Muriel Rukeyser. In truth, story in all its forms is at the heart of human culture in all times and places: it is one of the primary ways in which human beings seek to comprehend the world, the actual grain of human experience and the mystery of human destiny. Anne Loughnane's reclamation of the life story of her great-grandmother, Kate Corbett, reveals a truly astonishing tale which affirms that fact can often be stranger than fiction, and also that the life-path of the individual may be our best portal into the actuality of the past and by extension the diversity of the broader historical canvas. Everyone carries the imprint of other lived lives within their genes, like engendered ghosts whose near or distant dramas beckon from the dark within us and the limbo of lost record or witness. Historical record has tended to exclude or overlook women's lives in particular.

Kate Corbett's life defies all expectation or stereotype: a story of marriage and motherhood in post-Famine Dublin, against a backdrop of political struggle and agrarian agitation. There followed a traumatic transatlantic migration by the family to New York State, with the loss of two small children through illness en route and then the experience of rabid anti-Catholic-Irish prejudice on arrival. This in turn was to lead to a further family migration and settlement in Wyoming, with all its associated struggle, and the despatching of one of the children, a boy of eight, back to Ireland and his childless uncle in Clare.

There was to be a further astonishing turn in Kate Corbett's life story when, after she had raised her family and been widowed, she re-crossed the Atlantic and entered a Cistercian priory in England, where she would remain until her death thirteen years later.

Here is the most unusual story of an Irishwoman's life, its path uncovered and retraced by one of her descendents. Anne Loughnane sheds light not just on the life of the woman who was to be her great-grandmother, but in doing so leads us into a specific harbour of that other country which is the past. If we all carry human road-maps of that lost country darkly inscribed and embedded within us, then here is one such restored to light in the story of Kate Corbett.

Michael Coady is a poet and writer and a member of Aosdana, the affiliation of Irish artists under the aegis of the Arts Council of Ireland. His poem and prose sequence The Use of Memory, from his collection All Souls (Gallery Press 1997) unravels the story of his great-grandfather who emigrated to the United States, abandoning his young son.

CHAPTER [1]

Recollection Dublin
1841-1860

"Obey them that have the rule over you, and submit yourselves: for they watch for your souls,"

Hebrews Ch.. 13 Vs. 17

It was a fine cold day in early February when Reverend Mother summoned Kate to her study. The lovely crisp light spilled across the corner of the small oak table and onto the polished floor boards. Through the window she could glimpse the snow-drops with their promise of new life to lighten the Lenten days.

EVER SINCE she had embraced monastic life at the age of fifty-seven, Vincent visited his mother, Kate Corbett, once a year. It was a long and tedious journey from his farm near the village of Quin in Clare to the obscure Cistercian priory in rural Dorset, where she would live the enclosed life of the contemplative for the remainder of her days. He covered the weary miles by pony and trap, rail and steam-boat and, as often as not, strode the last few on foot. There, they would not touch, much less embrace. They would converse through a small wooden grill (about nine by twelve inches) inset into the wall which separated the rooms in which they sat.

He was nineteen when he made that journey for the first time, and Kate felt more like a remote loving aunt than a mother to him. She had, after all, forfeited her right to real filial feeling when she had sent him into the care of his aunt and uncle at the age of barely eight.

He had been daunted by the austerity of the parlour he was led into on the occasion of that first visit. The stark walls were adorned only by a rather forlorn picture of a little band of nuns wandering homeless across Europe fleeing persecution. He found himself fighting a rising sense of panic as he waited for the soft sound of the panel which screened the grill to be withdrawn.

Kate too had been apprehensive prior to that first visit. Over the previous year – her first in monastic life – she had become aware of a deepening sense of joy. She had tried to detach from worldly loves and interests and to empty herself of their noise, and this had borne fruit. She was grateful for an increasing appetite for poverty and solitude. Now, she feared that Vincent's visits would threaten her hard won sense of peace. Yet it was Kate herself who had suggested that he might like to know about her early life in Dublin and that of his father John Jo. She had been moved to compassion by his uneasiness as she glimpsed his faintly hunted expression through the grill and felt, rather than heard, the nervous tapping of his knees. She had sought to put him at his ease and he had seized gratefully on the suggestion. Thereafter she had been taken unaware by the torrent of memories unleashed by his questioning.

Reverend Mother was very aware of her fears and very gentle with her, but she believed that Vincent had a right to much of the information he sought. She had prayed about it, and was inclined to think that the story of Kate's journey to God could be not only a source of comfort to Vincent but of support to other souls seeking to make this journey. She therefore required her, in obedience, to respond fully to his questions, reminding her of the need for detachment from spiritual as well as sensual pleasures.

His first query about her early life in Dublin had taken Kate back a long way, and her memory of that time had a fragmented, dream-like quality. More than anything, it seemed to her then, a kaleidoscope of images and sounds: sounds of horse-drawn carriages and cabs rattling over the cobblestones, the calls and banter of the cabmen, the cries of flower sellers and hawkers in the street and, of course, the growing crescendo of beggary as hordes of starving men and women fled from the famine stricken countryside into the city.

There were also sounds of revelry and fun. The arc that linked St. Stephens Green and College green was one of continual exuberance created by the antics of the students from the colleges at either end. The excited murmurings of well-off shoppers, as they devoured the latest fashions and shimmering fabrics, percolated along Grafton Street. She recalled listening with mounting excitement for the chug-chugging of the steam train which took them from Westland Row to Sandymount beach. There, the cries of the gulls would mingle with the calls and screams of children and, more often than not, with the cry of the wind as well.

The more urgent childhood memories, both magical and fearful, came to mind too: her toes were so cold, she could see them whitely through the clear water. The jam jar was lodged firmly between two stones, and a large minnow was edging near it. Please God let it go in she had prayed ... she caught the jar and hugged it to herself in ecstasy. A darker memory came unbidden. She must have been about nine; they were picnicking with their cousins by the Dodder. Jim grinned – "Here you are Kate." She stood rooted in terror, as he extended the oily glistening eel. She had been indifferent to the hot shameful liquid trickling down her legs, and Jim, embarrassed, had turned away.

There were graver sounds when the men met together; after dinner when her father would speak with his friends about the huge turnouts at Daniel O'Connell's "monster meetings" or the chances of the repeal movement achieving dissolution of the Union. Their admiration for the achievements of "the Liberator", as O'Connell was known, was unbounded, as was their pride in him as an Irishman, and as a Catholic. Similar discussions could be heard from groups of men gathering after Mass on Sunday. As she got older, she became aware of more muted talk about the resurgence of Fenianism and the escalating violence of the land war in the countryside. The sense of foreboding would sometimes communicate itself to her, and she would need reassurance to quieten her fears.

These sounds were mirrored by images and smells; smells in particular seemed so evocative to Kate. The horses and bowler-hatted cabmen were everywhere, as was the astringent smell of fresh horse dung, gathered as quickly as it was dropped, and the strong tang of their urine. She recalled the smell of a red-nosed old man bending down to whisper to her, and whimpering "That's sore Mammy" as her mother whisked her away. The waft of stale porter mingling with sawdust, as a pub door swung open, accompanied strolls down most side streets. How she had relished the smell of roasting chestnuts of a winter's evening, and the smell of charcoal from the brazier. More than anything, she could remember the wonderful smells of food to the hungry appetite, the irresistible aroma of bacon and sausages sizzling in the pan, the basting smells of golden roasts and, of course, freshly baked bread and cakes.

Kate had loved the calm with which the lamplighter worked his nightly magic on their square. He would reach up with his long cane and leave a glowing trail of lamps in his wake, and the dull grey of the square would be transformed in the golden haze of their light. There were soldiers everywhere then, and the colours of their uniforms splashed across the grey streets. When the military bands played in St Stephen's Green or Kingstown, as they often did, Dublin had seemed full of a marvellous exhilaration. Fashionably dressed ladies and gentlemen were to be seen strolling all around them in St Stephen's Green, and along Grafton street, and she had delighted in their elegant air of ease and their beautiful gowns. The peak of fashionable effervescence occurred during the drawing room season, when the country's remaining debutantes descended on Dublin to be presented to the Lord Lieutenant, and the city centre fairly quivered in French silks and satins, delicate lace and sensual velvets. Kate and her sister Elisa spent hours gazing at the elegant broughams and carriages streaming into St Stephen's Green from neighbouring Mount Street and Fitzwilliam Square, and converging on the Shelbourne Hotel, which remained alight with frenzied festive activity for the duration, and of which they had a great view from their dining room window.

Alongside this pageant of colour and gaiety, there was another, of grim and desperate poverty. The workhouses and prisons were overflowing with the destitute, who, unmindful of the insalubrious conditions, frequently turned to crime to win the shelter and food of prison. Battered and emaciated men in rags roamed the streets, and in every nook and cranny of the city were huddled skeletal women and their thin children, begging.

She remembered one occasion, passing Dublin Castle with Nan, their housekeeper, and a long queue of the starving awaiting their turn for some sort of soup. "Why have they chained the mug to the big pot?" she had asked Nan "They're afraid the poor craturs will run away with their dirty oul mug," she answered, and Kate had been surprised to see her crying quietly. Nan later told her mother that two of her cousins were among those waiting for a mug of soup. She had felt obscurely shamed, watching the well fed bodies of the supervising soldiers encased in the colours of their regiment. She recalled the searing image of hundreds of gaunt skeletal figures lined up on the quays, waiting to be transported to the ships anchored further out, and a memory of her father lifting her up to see the tall masts, which, he said, were beacons of hope for those people seeking to sail to a better life in the new world.

As a child, Kate accepted that her world was encompassed by these contrasting images. She did not then cast judgement but, as was natural for a child, turned when she could, away from such dark misery to the more seductive brightness of gaiety and laughter. As she got older, she would accompany her mother in delivering parcels of food and clothing to the Sisters of Charity who looked after the poor and sick nearby in St Stephen's Green, and to the Sisters of Mercy in Baggott Street who cared for, and educated young women and poor or orphaned children, and her compassion for their plight grew. It was to be many more years before she could fully appreciate the horror that was visited upon her country's poor during those terrible years, or a sense of outrage at the injustice that had befallen them was to take root.

Nonetheless, she had a happy, carefree childhood. She remembered being fascinated by birds and used to pore over a beautifully illustrated book of her father's for hours on end. She recalled the delight with which she peeled back each fragile sheet of tissue paper, to reveal the delicate little beings who possessed that most enviable gift of flight. While she had relished the exotic and beautiful – the flamingos, birds of paradise and the awe inspiring condor, she loved best the robins, thrushes, finches and all the familiar birds that frequented their garden. She shared this passion with Nan, who never failed to put out pieces of fat and breadcrumbs on the window ledges of the kitchen and on the back lawn. Together, they would watch them as they fed, and Nan would tell her their names and all about their different habits.

Nan Loughlin had come to work for Kate's parents in the late 1820s, from a little village outside Kilkenny. Her family lost everything in the hungry years, when a harsh landlord, the tithe collector and her father's weakness for poitin reduced the family to near beggary. She had been recommended by the local schoolteacher – that same teacher who had imbued her with a love for birds during her too brief years of schooling. Though not overly fond of Kate, Nan was one of the constants of her childhood. Kate was too serious-minded and stiff a child to bring any ease to the sharp edge of life for her. Nan loved and was fiercely loyal to Kate's mother, whom she regarded, as having saved her from a life of poverty and misery. Her mother had a personality that was gay and kind, and this had warmed Nan's heart which had been too early shrivelled by bitter hardship. Though she tolerated her father, she was in general contemptuous of men, blaming her own father for bringing ruin on the family through drink. Knowing the hardship of life then, this was, Kate believed, too harsh a judgement.

Nan's stories and beliefs brought with them the whiff of an older Celtic Christian and even pagan world. There had been many a fearful tale of the "pooka", a sort of fairy spirit they would do well to be wary of. These were always abroad on stormy nights, rattling doors and windows, which terrified them as they huddled close to the kitchen fire. On February the first, she would sit them down at the kitchen table to make *brideogs* – images of St. Brigid dressed in lovely clothes. Next day, they would visit homes where Nan had a housekeeping or maid friend, and while not allowed to collect money as Nan would once have done, they had lovely tea parties.

Most exciting of all was the night of June the twenty third, St John's Eve, when a big bonfire was lit in the garden and there was a party to celebrate mid-summer. Kate's parents entered into this celebration with zest, and it became known as "Nan's Do". Aunt Jane, Uncle Charlie and cousins Jim and Geraldine, as well as family friend and neighbour Dr Corbett were always there, and Kate's eyes grew bright as she described the preparations for this event. Every floor and piece of furniture was polished. On the day itself, fires glowed and spat in the two reception rooms, and the gleaming mirrors reflected back the vases of cut flowers her mother loved so much. The large mahogany sideboard was set out with platters of cold roast chicken and ham and the spiced beef to which her father was partial, flanked by plates of thinly cut and buttered brown soda bread. It was the array of fruit flans, trifles and jellies that held the young ones in thrall. Kate would gaze mesmerised, at the sparkle and gleam of the cut glass decanters housing mysterious grown up substances, and the big floral jug of Nan's homemade lemonade, at which the children slaked their thirst. The excitement as they awaited the arrival of the first guests, and the clang of the front door knocker, was intense. Lucy, the maid, would take the gentlemen's and children's coats and hang them in the lower hall, while Nan brought the ladies upstairs to the visitors' room, where they re-powdered and where, it seemed to Kate, the rapture of the evening began.

Nan, then off duty for the evening, joined her friends in the kitchen, where a smaller, less ornate version of the upstairs feast was laid out.

Supper was served by Lucy and Aunt Jane's maid, lent for the occasion. After the pudding, the children, excused from the table, raced for the garden where old Joe, the gardener, had the bonfire in full swing. The usual games of "tig", and "hide and seek", were transformed in the spark-filled darkness, and it was with delicious terror that they rushed back from the ominous shadows to the comforting circle of light around the fire.

Gradually, as the light began to fade, their elders, with Nan and her friends, would join them. There must have been some rainy nights, but Kate could not remember them. What she did recall was the delight of roasting chestnuts in the embers of the ebbing fire, which still managed to pierce the encroaching night with little explosive sparks. There would be singing then, and the elegiac tones of her Uncle Charlie's *I Dreamt I Dwelt in Marble Halls* would fill the night air. The one they all waited for, was Nan's haunting rendition of the beautiful Irish song, *Sliabh Geall Gua*, a song from her own part of the country. She used to look so sad then, that it always made Kate want to cry. The best part of the evening was the end, when everyone had gone and, despite her mother's protests, her father would take her on his shoulders back into the garden, by then almost completely black, and point out the various constellations. Though she was to see many a magnificent star-studded night sky over the course of her life, none had touched her so deeply, as the wonder and loveliness of those early glimpses of the heavens on St John's Eve.

In response to Vincent's query, Kate said that she had not been particularly pious as a little girl. However, she described days punctuated at regular intervals by prayer and devotions; morning and evening prayer, before and after meals and, of course, the daily drama of stopping at twelve noon, and again at six to pray the Angelus. "This ensured," Kate told her son, "that we did not drift too far from a consciousness of Our Lord, and the great mystery of the Incarnation, at any point during the day." Other small devotions, such as dropping into the church for a few minutes' adoration before the Blessed Sacrament, and repeating frequent prayerful aspirations, were part of the pulse of daily life. Above all, there was the cycle of the Church's liturgical life which revolved around the great feasts of Christmas and Easter. "To ready ourselves for these," said Kate, "we had Advent and Lent, when habits of self denial instilled in us a sense of personal connection with Christ's redeeming sacrifice, and for us children, this meant, giving up sweets and lemonade". For her, this had been a faint foretaste of the powerful spiritual expectancy which these liturgical events later came to hold for her.

She recalled, as a child, the bleakness of Good Friday mirrored in the altar of their local church stripped bare, and the plain wooden cross flanked by candles. Kate and her mother would shuffle prayerfully around the lonely stations of the cross alongside others of the devout. While she did not, then, have the subtle depths of Gregorian chant to discover the full colour and warmth of the exultant Easter liturgy, she did have a sense of the gladness of the occasion. This had been conveyed by the brilliant wash of colour from flowers and vestments, and everywhere there were new Easter outfits and hats. All of this, alongside the bells and the triple alleluias ringing out over Dublin city, marked the end of the long fast and gave promise of joys to come.

More than anything, Kate had relished Sunday afternoon devotions, to which her Mother took her faithfully every

week, and it is to these that she traced the earliest roots of her
vocation to the contemplative life. In Dublin as elsewhere in
Europe these decades were marked by a huge upsurge in the
devotional life of the Church, and this clearly impacted on
Kate's life. She loved the thunderous sound of the rosary
washing over her, as the congregation responded as one to the
lone voice of the priest who led it. She felt swept along in
safety by the tremendous surge of the responses, and doubly
soothed by the stillness of the quiet adoration that followed.
Most magical of all for Kate had been the beautiful ceremony
of benediction that ended the devotions. Then the Sanctuary
would glow she said, with a multitude of candles, and the red
and white surpliced acolytes would lead the priest to the altar.
The whiff of incense, accompanied by the soft sound of the
thurible, would waft towards her, before the swell of the or-
gan introduced the solemn *0 Salutaris Hostia* and the choir
gave full voice to that most beautiful of all the great hymns to
the Eucharist, the *Tantum Ergo*.

Kate always conveyed a sense of the spiritual and even
sensual beauty of such ceremonies though she had not then
been conscious of them in these terms. She just knew that she
liked going, and had been aware of a sense of stillness tinged
with awe.

She described herself as a rather bookish little girl at home,
and a bit of a tomboy when out playing with Elisa and her
cousins. "You will be shocked to hear," she told Vincent, "that
I was, on occasion, capable of spectacular sins." She could still
see the delicate pale blue gloves and the long tangerine silk
scarf, which she had stolen from her cousin Geraldine, and
recalled vividly the salutary sense of shame that followed
discovery." The searing phrases remained with her; 'How
could you Kate, and Geraldine so fond of you ....' She had been
glad of the dark in the confessional – her hands clutched tightly
to stop the trembling: 'I confess ...' "Oh, the blessed relief" she
had fairly skipped from the Church, restored to God's Grace
and decency. Kate had always been thankful for the sacrament

of confession, which she regarded, as a wonderful provision to enable us to slough off the dead weight of sin.

Kate had dearly loved her father, and recalled with great fondness their Sunday morning walks after Mass. He loved the stretch of canal between the bridges of Leeson and Baggot Street, and there they would watch the golden ducklings in early spring, the quirky busy moorhens in summer, and admire the elegance with which the beautiful swans graced the modest canal. But most of all she delighted in the magical way the barges navigated the narrow locks. "Look Daddy, the boat has been sucked away," he would smile as she watched, astonished, to see it slowly reappear further down.

Her father it was who had comforted that hidden well of loneliness which arose from her awareness of being somehow less than satisfactory for her mother, a sense which her mother would not have wanted to convey, but nevertheless felt. She could remember with gratitude overhearing his slightly irritated response to her mother's disclosure of the thieving episodes: "For God's sake, Mary Anne, there is no need to make such heavy weather of it; many children take things from time to time, and God knows, if you did not always make so much of Geraldine and how lovely she looks, the chances are that Kate would not even have noticed the wretched things."

So she had grown up for the most part in easy contentment in a lovely home, blessed with food, warmth, faith and books, and with sufficient love and care. Her world had moved gradually outward to embrace the park and surrounding streets, and in due course, school life with the Loreto nuns across the Green. Here, companioned by Geraldine and Elisa life was pleasant and congenial. She liked the calm order of the daily routine, and her studies came easily. She had a particular aptitude for languages and music, and though neither as pretty nor as popular as Elisa or Geraldine, she found a niche for herself through her music, and was always in demand as an accompanist or as a member of musical ensembles.

It was not until Kate had reached the age of fifteen or sixteen, when the ominous "future" began to loom, that her faith became central to her life. She had been drawn to the excitement of adventure and foreign travel and was loth to don the passive role of Victorian young womanhood. The acquisition of the feminine arts of domestic management, fine needlework and charitable visits held no allure for her. She regarded with some panic the prospect of years of embroidery and the preparation of food parcels, stretching ahead of her, and even her father seemed to assume that she would enter with enthusiasm into these dismal tasks.

It was then that she began to think of the religious life and particularly that of a missionary, which seemed to offer exciting prospects of travel, and possibly danger. Besides which, this was a choice which neatly sidestepped the uncomfortable challenge of learning to deal with "men". Elisa and Geraldine had been much less troubled by this, and indeed were already on friendly terms with a number of young men. They were incredulous when Kate first spoke of her burgeoning interest in the religious life, unable to conceive, they said, "how anyone would want to bury themselves alive". Kate had relished in private the thought of her vocation, and found it a wonderful distraction from the loneliness which had begun to dog these years. She found herself visited by an increasing faith in God, and was able to respond serenely to all the demands of her life, even those uncongenial tasks which she began to look on as training in self-denial. Her prayer life intensified and she would go to chapel half an hour earlier in the morning to try and meditate. She would stop by the little Byzantine church attached to the new university, each evening on her way home from school, where she loved the colourful mosaics that adorned the walls. Surrounded by their splendour, the "rightness" of the religious life had seemed very apparent to her.

Life during those years was a busy round of social gatherings, in the homes of family and friends. As a musician, Kate had been much in demand, and her social confidence increased as her terror of young men reduced. Indeed she gradually developed a growing circle of friends and acquaintances, and surprised in herself a certain wit and humour that seemed to please. There were some wonderful nights at the Theatre Royal and the Fishamble Street Music Academy, and the intensity of her religious life began to wane slightly under such a barrage of worldly delights.

It was around this time that she first mentioned to her parents that she had been thinking of the religious life. Her mother was as astounded as Elisa and Geraldine had been, unable to conceive as "desirable", a way of life so alien to what she herself could embrace. It was however her father's disappointment that she minded most. She could still recall his words: "Kate I do not believe that God would want you to take such a momentous step without being fully aware of what you are doing. You need a fuller experience of life and the world, and I want you to defer making such a decision for at least two years."

Well, she could not bear to hurt this kindly man, who had so sheltered her young and vulnerable self, and she readily agreed to his request. She was, if truth be told, a little relieved to make this promise. While not acknowledging it to herself, Kate's appetite for religious life had been reducing in direct proportion to her increasing delight in worldly life. She began to take an interest in her appearance, and in dress and fashion which gave her mother a lot of pleasure. She had also become aware that she was not unattractive to the young men she met socially, and then of course, she met John Jo, but more of that anon.

CHAPTER [2]

Young Love and Parting Dublin 1860-1862

"Blessed is he that considereth the poor: the Lord will deliver him in time of trouble."

Psalm 41 Vs. 1

When allocated the task of scrubbing the kitchen floor, Kate would gladly offer up her aches and stiffness for Nan and Lucy, and the many others whose labour cushioned her young life in Dublin and whose care she then took for granted.

KATE AND JOHN JO were young when they first met. She was but lately gone twenty one and he was some months younger. It was at a musical supper in the home of Dr Corbett who lived near them in St Stephen's Green. She remembered the night well...the skies, banked heavily over the trees in the park as they set out, augured snow, and the light cast by the gas lamps was more opaque than usual. The beautiful fanlight over Dr Corbett's front door was alight, and the warmth of his welcome banished the chill of the evening.

Kate loved their evenings in his elegant drawing room. The generous fire breathed its heat into all corners, illuminating the polished boards and rich colours of the Turkish rugs. The soft light from the many lamps glowed deeply in the warm varnish of the finely wrought, inlaid furniture – Dr. Corbett and her father shared a passion for fine woodwork. That particular night he was entertaining them alongside relatives of his, one of whom was young John Jo Corbett, and the other a cousin, Father Dan, a diocesan priest from Clare up on a week's holiday. She remembered watching through the window the snowflakes suspended in the gaslight before dropping lightly to carpet the pavement, and bathing the evening in a hushed glow. Their images, reflected in the lovely oval mirror over the mantel, were strangely still.

Everyone seemed tinged with a faint beauty that night. Kate's father, rotund and of low stature, looked well in his fine silk waistcoat and handsome gold fob watch. Her mother, who was a big woman, was stately in a dark blue silk dress with ivory lace at throat and cuffs. Elisa's appearance, as always, was vivid. She was a slim, fine boned girl with an arresting combination of auburn hair and slate blue eyes. Though her lower face was a little heavy, the sparkle and gaiety of her personality conveyed an enduring sense of remarkable prettiness. That night she was dressed in a pale blue silk dress with a panel of darker blue satin tapering into her neat waist. Kate took after her mother and was taller, with a larger frame. She was however a slender young woman then, and the green velvet of her skirt suited her pale skin and caught the greenish fleck in her hazel eyes. Over it she wore a close fitting cream silk jacket with little pearl buttons.

John Jo was last to arrive. His vigorous scraping on the doorstep stilled the conversation and she caught a glimpse of the light fringe of snow on his jacket before the maid took it and he entered the room with Father Dan. His vitality was immediately apparent, and his slight athletic frame seemed to her "all energy" while that of his cousin seemed all "measured caution". The evening changed then; the pleasant languor of their earlier welcome evaporated, and it seemed as if, suddenly, all were on the alert. "God save all here" he called, his soft Clare accent belying the vigour of his greeting, "I got delayed at the Eagle Tavern putting the last touches to next months edition of the *Nation*."

Kate remembered the uneasy pause; Father Dan said, "John Jo, you need to watch your step or you could loose your job. The government will not take kindly to the fomentation of unrest among their own employees". "Devil the bit of danger" came the response in that carefree tone she came to know so well. He paused at the entry to the drawing room, and apologised on seeing them, for bringing politics, as he said, "to weary the party." He had a lean dark face that was sombre in repose, but infectiously merry when he smiled, which he did then. He bowed gravely to the ladies and shook hands with Kate's father, and they all tucked into an appetising supper, of which, she could later only recall the lobster salad and a tasty pear and almond flan.

The light from the fire and the lamps sparkled on cut glass decanters and on the elegant long stemmed glasses from which they drank their moselle cup. John Jo was very assured even as a young man and drew Elisa and Kate into the conversation, and she remembered that they laughed a lot. Elisa was very quick witted and the banter between John Jo and her was pleasant and humorous.

Kate did become aware as the evening wore on that he was particularly attentive to her, and she began even then to fall under his spell a little. As always, the party finished with music, and John Jo stood by the piano as Kate ran her fingers over the yellowing keys and launched into a frolicsome minuet by Mozart. She enjoyed the round of songs with which the night ended, as much for the quirkiness of personality revealed as for the music. Her mother's thin and quavery voice nearly always sounded faintly out of tune, and her relief when she concluded *The Blackbird* without collapse, was touchingly matched by her pleasure at having done so. Dr Corbett's poignant *Believe me of all those endearing young charms* brought tears to Elisa's eyes, and her father's rendering of the simple haunting air of *Eileen Aroon,* which he sang with total absorption, brought a quiet to the company. John Jo soon banished this when he reduced them all to laughter with a lengthy traditional dance tune which he accompanied by dancing a jig without the flicker of a smile!

By then, Kate had settled into a pleasant round of life in west St Stephen's Green. She loved the early morning sounds of the horse-drawn trams and cabs over the cobbles. Her father had a business, manufacturing patent blinds and bath-chairs that included cabinet making and upholstery workshops. The showrooms where the goods were on display were on the ground floor and the workshops were in the offices around the back of the building. They lived overhead in the spacious Georgian rooms of the second and third floors and Nan and Lucy had their rooms in the attic.

Alert to the muffled sounds of the shutters opening and the workers arrival, Kate and her father were always first down and breakfasted together. They would then descend to the shop floor to oversee the opening of a new day of business. She took particular pleasure in the woods and varnishes of the cabinet making workshops, and the comic banter of Jimjo Tierney and Jack Farrell who worked there. Miss Edgeworth, a careful Protestant lady of reduced circumstances, presided over the glowing vibrant colours of the upholstery department, assisted by Miss O Neill, a second cousin of her mother's. She loved to show customers around the business and was gladdened by their appreciation of the fine handiwork on offer. Kate's mother felt that it was unbecoming in a young woman to be so closely involved with the business, but her father took pleasure in her interest and it strengthened the bond between them.

The afternoons and evenings followed a predictable pattern of visits to relatives and friends, and afternoon devotions on Fridays and Sundays in the beautiful new Church of St Andrews in Westland Row, where she sang in the choir.

There, she was involved with a group of young women in raising funds for the poor through concerts and musical evenings. These were held in the Antient Concert Rooms and the Fishamble Street Music Theatre, where she was regularly called upon to play the piano, or accompany artistes. The daily round was enlivened by house parties or concerts and dramatic productions in the homes of friends or at the theatre, and in spring and summer by outings to the seaside or races.

John Jo brought an invigorating if slightly disturbing element to her days. He admired the Young Ireland movement which had splintered away from Daniel O'Connell's Repeal Association. This had espoused non-violence as part of its creed but the Young Irelanders were given to more insurrectionist rhetoric, and rallied around *The Nation* newspaper. This alarmed Kate's father and his older friends who, staunchly Catholic and Nationalistic, were devoted to O'Connell and fearful that the young hotheads would plunge the country into violence and destruction.

John Jo had witnessed fearful images while growing up in his native Clare during the famine years - images of corpses strewn in ditches and starving children were to haunt him right up to the time of his death. The anger born of this fuelled a passion against the injustice of poverty. He believed that the emerging Fenianist movement was addressing this more vigorously than the Repeal movement, of whose slower constitutional methods he was impatient.

They began to see each other fairly frequently in the homes of mutual friends, and at outings to the theatre and concert halls. Kate's parents liked him very much in spite of their reservations about his political leanings. They did not regard his growing friendship with their daughter seriously, seeing them both as very young and John Jo, as they said, "with his way to make in the world". Indeed her father in particular was very glad to see her having such fun and relished the high spirits that characterized their gatherings. He cherished the hope that all notion of religious life was a thing of the past, and that she was settling down to what he regarded as a more "normal" life for a girl. There were certain aspects of the faith that he was uneasy about, and religious life for women was one of them. Neither her mother or sister thought that there was anything out of the ordinary about her relationship with John Jo at that time. He got on very well with both of them, sharing a delight in humorous banter, at which all three were very good.

However she was aware from very early on, that John Jo's feelings for her ran more deeply than was apparent, and became troubled by this. His banter was very much gentler with her, for she did not have a facility in wit, though she appreciated it in others, and loved it when he made her laugh as he did so much. He also shared with her his feelings of anger and outrage at what he saw as the indifference of the government, and indeed the well off Catholic classes to the awful destitution that surrounded them. She remembered meeting him one evening as she returned from benediction at the Pro-Cathedral- she was very aware that he planned his religious devotions at that time to coincide with hers. He brought her around by Mountjoy square, and there, the starving and destitute swarmed around discarded elegant houses whose paintwork was peeling and in some cases the windows and fanlights were broken. Barefoot children, hardly covered in rags, played fitfully in the gaslight and emaciated women just stared or spoke desultorily to one another, sometimes holding a bundle of rags that hid an infant, or a half jam jar of what looked like weak porter. The men stood apart singly, seeming too defeated even for conversation.

"There are twelve or more people living in each room of those buildings Kate," John Jo told her, "they are often without a fire and rely on old papers or straw for warmth. It is not right." He spoke of his friend, Jo Costelloe, who worked with the local parish priest to try and bring some relief, and who affirmed that most of these poor folk were decent and good living; many had fled the famine in the country to try and make a living in the city. They would work if they could, but there was no work for them. "I'm ashamed to say that I could not do it Kate", he told her, "I tried once or twice, but the smells got to me...smells of sickness, rotting straw and stale porter. I had to be sick."

Kate was shocked, though God knows she knew that the city was full of hunger and misery, but somehow she had never had to look at it so directly, and had probably unconsciously avoided those streets where it was most visible. John Jo, realising her distress was conscience-stricken, and berated himself for showing her what so clearly preoccupied him. "Hush John Jo, I am glad you did" she told him, for indeed she felt that it was a chastening mirror to the ease of her own life which she took for granted. She spoke to him a little, about the work of the Sisters of Mercy in Baggot street, who cared for poor or orphaned children and young women which she admired. She met up with other young women there once a week, to make clothes for the children and plan fund raising events. It was then also that she told him for the first time about her leanings towards the religious life. He stopped in the street and looked so stricken, that involuntarily she put her hand up to touch his face. "But I want to marry you Kate, surely you know that," he said, and she found that she could bear his pain even less than the misery all around her. His vulnerability wrung from her a tenderness she did not know she possessed. She recalled that he kept hold of her hand, and asked if she had any feelings for him at all. At this she put her other hand in his, and told him that she had but that she was confused and troubled. "I know that I will have to make my way and convince your father that I can provide for you," he continued, "but I will do it Kate, if only you'll have me," and he finished simply, "if you find you cannot marry me, I do not believe I could ever replace you."

Kate was in turmoil. While a preoccupation with her vocation had become fainter since leaving school, she still assumed that she would return to it. In addition to the question of her vocation there was the difficulty of her parents' views. She was very aware that John Jo's suit would not be welcomed by them. He was a young man in a lowly governmental job offering limited prospects. Besides which, his political leanings and those of his associates made them anxious, an anxiety compounded by his habit of meeting up in public houses such as the Brazen Head and the Eagle tavern where Fenian sympathisers foregathered. Her parents believed that this lifestyle, alongside his convivial personality, put him at grave risk of forming habits of excessive drinking, which would be inimical to domestic peace and family life. She knew that her father, in his fondness for John Jo, had already advised him to withdraw from these associates, but though respectful and attentive to him, John Jo would not do so.

Kate was aware from the beginning that she would not give up her love for John Jo in spite of all the obstacles. "Undoubtedly," she told Vincent, "my soul was frail then, and I suppose all our youthful energy yearned towards each other." She had, she said, a profound sense of ease and homecoming when with him, and in his acknowledged need of her, which drew forth her most tender feelings. She did worry that she was resisting God's will, and described the feverish internal dialogue with which she was wracked for weeks – surely God would not place in her heart such a love, only to torment John Jo and herself by denying it fulfilment? The corresponding taunt, "what about dying to self and subjugating the desires of the flesh to achieve a higher spiritual good?" would follow, and so it went on without resolution. In the end she spoke to an old priest, Father Cusack, who used to say daily Mass in Clarendon street where she sometimes went. He listened gravely, smiling faintly at the mulish tone with which she asserted that she could not give up John Jo. Father Cusack told her with some asperity: "My dear girl, if your vocation was for the religious life, you would want that more than anything." Clearly you do not, so try and serve Our Lord in what is an equally challenging vocation, that of forming and sustaining a Christian family in his service." As Kate asserted, it was as well that she did not then know the journey that was in front of her. Had she done so, her joy and relief at hearing these words would very likely have been more muted. As it was, she felt that the additional obstacle of her parents' opposition was little by comparison.

It was some weeks before they had the opportunity to speak together again. When they did, it was at Sandymount beach, where they were picnicking with her cousins. They drove out in a horse drawn cab, along streets veiled, she recalled, in the fresh green of early Summer, and alive with masses of cherry blossom. Slightly chilled from the brisk ride, they raced each other across the ebbed sand. They could discern the thin white edge of foam far out, and beyond it the open sea and they made for this. Elisa, Jim and Geraldine were way ahead when John Jo asked Kate to slow down. He called to the others, "we're going to explore the sandbanks for a sheltered spot for the picnic," and they waved and nodded. She could see the Martello tower squat and defiant to their left and beyond it the beautiful mountains of Dublin and Wicklow.

"Kate, have you thought any more about what I said," he asked her, and his face, she recalled, was taut and apprehensive. She told him that she had, and that she knew she wanted to marry him. He was very pale, and he did not smile with delight as she had expected. They had reached the sandbanks and he sat down and covered his face in his hands. Kate became alarmed as he seemed ill, but when she asked him he looked up with great tenderness and stood up. "I had braced myself for a no Kate, as I had not allowed myself to hope since last I met you," he said. There were tears in his eyes, and she remembered wondering at her power to call forth such love, and feeling a bit frightened by it. They stood and he took her in his arms and held her to him stroking her hair. She smiled when she remembered that she wanted to stay there forever.

The others were nearing then and Kate and John Jo turned to meet them and busied themselves settling in to a secluded trough amongst the hillocks of coarse sand. They picnicked on thickly-cut ham sandwiches pungent with mustard and some cold chicken pieces followed by Nan's delicious fruit and almond cake, washed down with bottles of porter for the men and lemonade for the girls. Ever afterwards the gritty taste of sand in food would recall the magic of that picnic for her. At about three in the afternoon the air chilled and they could see the fog gathering out at sea. It quickly curled around them as they made their way back over the sea wall, and the light from the gas lamps dissolved eerily above their heads.

John Jo and Kate lingered behind to talk. They were well aware that they would not be able to marry for a long time. Her parents would not consent unless they were confident that John Jo could support a family. Kate's father believed that his prospects would improve if he were to seek a transfer to the Indian service, as he knew that young Catholic men would find it hard to advance in Dublin as senior posts were in the hands of Protestants who distrusted Catholics, particularly at that time because of the rise of Fenianism within the city, and the spread of agrarian violence throughout the countryside.

John Jo looked thoughtful as he and Kate discussed this. "I have actually thought about doing this," he said, "and in fact if I had not met you I might have done so by now. The job I do is deathly tame and I can see little chance of advancement, but it is a long way, Kate, and the chances are that we would be separated for at least five years." She did not say then, that her parents also worried about his involvement in the radical politics that circulated in the clubs he frequented.

John Jo enjoyed the social life and comradeship of these, but Kate worried about the drinking involved, and the danger of developing habits it would be more difficult to break later. She dearly loved him but she was not blind to his failings, though her conviction, that his many endearing qualities and admirable traits greatly outweighed these, was never to waver in spite of all the hardships she endured. He had a warm affectionate nature and his delight in life meant that it was very hard for him to resist the lure of fun. It was both his strength and weakness to live "in the moment" without too much thought for the morrow. On occasion he spent too much time drinking with his friends, and, of course, passionate as he was about justice, it was easy to be carried away by the political rhetoric that could lead to violence. Kate did not say any of this to him, not wanting to evoke that stubborn obstinacy of which he was also capable. John Jo had a young mans loyalty to his friends, however rash or misguided their behaviour. She knew however, that if he approached her parents with a plan to go to India for at least five years to forge a career for himself that they would look more kindly on his suit. Though unhappy at the thought of the long separation, John Jo could appreciate the need for it, and indeed the excitement of the adventure in prospect greatly reconciled him to its inevitability.

He duly approached her father, who, after some resistance on the grounds of their youth and lack of means, eventually agreed to them writing. There was to be no formal engagement, he said, but if they were both of the same mind and John Jo had the means to support a family after five years, her parents would agree to their marrying.

A bare three months later they said goodbye at Kingstown. It was a dismal night towards the end of summer with the harbour and city again encased in fog and the sound of the foghorn punctuating the damp stillness with its morose toll.

The previous evening he had dined with Kate's family in St Stephen's Green and her parents and Elisa went for a walk after dinner, leaving them to spend a last hour together. They relished the rare happiness of such intimacy in the warm glow of the fire and lamplight: it was enough to be together. They reassured each other that the time would pass quickly and that they would write regularly. John Jo, buoyed up with the adventure of it all, was much less sad than Kate. He was after all a young man who had found his days in the Registry of Deeds office very dull indeed, so it was not surprising that the thought of seeing a "bit of life" should be attractive, and indeed she envied him and would truly have loved to have gone with him, but of course that was out of the question. He knew her sadness and held her close while she cried a little. Then he was gone.

CHAPTER [3]

Dublin illumined by India and darkened by death 1862-1867

"I have been young, and now am old; yet have I not seen the righteous forsaken, nor his seed begging bread."

Psalm 37 Vs. 25

Kate watched Sister Peter's thin body, wrapped in the cowl of her habit, being lowered reverently into the grave. There, she was received into the hands of Sister Veronica and Sister Humbeline and laid on the earth while the choir sang the glorious *chorus angelorum*. If there were times when it was hard to live as a Cistercian nun, she could say with all sincerity that it was easy to die there.

FOR KATE those next few weeks were strangely dream like; then, four weeks later, the first of his letters arrived and for the next five years, there drifted into their staid Dublin home the colours, sounds and scents of an unimaginably different world. The local beeches and elms paled by comparison with the cork and brilliantly flowering jacaranda trees and the mango, banana and coconut groves. The extravagance of colour was everywhere. Cerise, orange, purple and magenta bougainvillaea cascading over walls and climbing trees, hedges of poinsettia hot and red, and of plumbago in pale blue. Flower beds were full of huge chrysanthemums in bronze, yellow, white and pink, red streaked amaryllis lilies, hibiscus and passion flowers. An initially alien landscape gradually became familiar. Kate could envision jute and rice fields stretching flatly to the horizon, patrolled by white paddy birds and vultures, rivers a mile wide where kites and kingfishers made their home, dappled sunshine that filtered through the shade trees bordering the acres of tea bushes and the deft delicacy of the tea pluckers at work. "I caught and killed a cobra about five feet long," he wrote casually in a letter littered with references to mosques, hindu temples and bazaars. She became used to images of babus dressed in white muslin, patient silent bullocks working the wheels that drew the water from the wells, burning funeral pyres and sacred cows allowed to roam at will. She wondered what the spicy stews and mulligatawny soup he seemed so fond of, tasted like, and remembered enquiring of their local grocer if he ever sold ghee butter or mustard oil, to that poor man's bemusement. She delighted in descriptions of the wonderful Hindu festivals of light and colour *Diwali* and *Holi,* and of the coming of the monsoon rains.

There were dark times too. She recalled a lengthy period of silence some five or six months after he left her when her initial pique gave way to anxiety as the weeks turned into months. He was stationed at Lahore in the plains of Punjab at that time and his picturesque descriptions of that city with its huge open square surrounded by arched cloisters, where the fierce Afghan and Pathan tribesmen foregathered with their horse and camel caravans, began to assume a more sinister aspect.

His letter, when it did arrive, spoke of long weeks in an abyss of fever and listlessness: "You cannot imagine what the heat is like Kate, I can only liken it to living in a furnace, with no escape inside or out, even though every shutter is kept tightly closed against the sun. It is impossible to sleep. Sometimes I manage a kind of fitful rest by keeping a bucket of water by me and pouring jugfuls over my body through the night. Sometimes I just get up and prowl the city until dawn. It is then that the city is reclaimed by its own people, when at midnight you hear the clarion cry of the muezzin calling the people to prayer from the Minar of the Wahir Khan mosque, and watch the sea of bodies rise up in response, you realise, Kate, that you are a foreigner in their land. Well I was already half crazed with the heat when I got some kind of an insect bite on my neck which became hugely inflamed and swollen. I became very feverish and was taken to Lahore hospital for treatment, and to be honest, I did not care whether I lived or died. Apparently, I had a nasty dose of what's called the 'Lahore sore'. It has taken me these six weeks to get my health back and I am determined not to spend another hot weather season in the plains as I believe it would kill me."

It was about two months later he wrote, "I am moving to a little hill station just outside Darjeeling to take up post as manager of a tea estate owned by a Scotsman Mr Campbell. There, the climate is more temperate and the hot weather when it comes is diluted by monsoons and torrential thunderstorms. I will live on the estate in a nice little bungalow with green shutters and a verandah. I am mighty glad to be getting away from this accursed heat."

She became familiar with the cheery personality of Maila Singh, his cook and houseman, and the more taciturn one of Abdullah the gardener and odd job man. "Kate, you'll need to learn to cook like Maila," he wrote, "his chicken and rice dishes and vegetable patties are mouth-watering. I have come to love this spicy food, which makes our own seem so pallid." Maila also cleaned, polished and ironed for him and he would tease her about the high expectations he would have when they married.

She loved his accounts of the quiet starlit nights when he slept out on the verandah. "All around the silence was so thick, punctuated only by the baying of jackals from the forests behind us, and the sporadic bursts of cicada calls, but I was not lonely Kate. I looked up through my mosquito net at those same stars that you can see from your back garden and I felt close to you," and of course, she worried about his not infrequent bouts of dysentery.

In Lahore much of his social life had revolved around "the club", where he was active in amateur dramatic and musical performances, and enjoyed the riding and tennis parties and what he called *pagal khanas,* picnics to places of interest. However there was often little to do and Kate worried about what he acknowledged to be a pattern of too great reliance on drink. She was relieved when, in Darjeeling he met up with some kindred spirits. "I have met some great people, Kate - an Edinburgh couple Neil and Maude Kerr who run the dispensary here and two formidable Sotswomen from Dundee, Ishbel and Jane Nicholl who are in charge of the local primary school. Many of the high and mighty of the land come here for the season because of the climate, but it has been a relief to meet such admirable and down to earth folk. We have some very convivial evenings exchanging tunes and stories. Neil is a fiddler and a great Robbie Burns fan and Maude is a wonderful singer". He promised to teach her the words of *A Man's a Man for A' That* when he returned. It should be "the anthem of the world" he said. Though they liked what Neil called "a wee dram", he reassured her that Maude was a strong minded woman and kept an eye on them.

It was some four years after he left Dublin that, he wrote to say, "I have been approached by a group of rich tea planters from Assam and Darjeeling, who are concerned about the ravages wrought by tigers on livestock and in some cases on villagers around their estates. They have offered me a contract as "dangerous game hunter" on very favourable terms, with the option of returning to my present post afterwards, which I have decided to accept Kate."

The lure of such an exciting project would have been irresistible to John Jo. He had learnt to shoot as a young boy in Clare and was an excellent horseman. He greatly relished not only the excitement of the hunt but also the opportunity to travel all over the foothills of the Himalayas in east and west

Bengal. Kate was torn between a vicarious enjoyment of his adventures and an awful fear for his safety. She recalled a remarkable account in one of his letters from that time.

"We spent three days in the forests around the village Kate, trying to get some trace of the man-eating tiger that had snatched a small child just six weeks before, but without success. On the evening of the third day, I took my gun and strolled into the jungle along a narrow path from the village, at about five o'clock. The growth was thick on either side and the evening sun had flung a zebra pattern of light and shade across the path. I thought I'd try my hand at a tiger bark that I had been practising, and when I did, wasn't there an answering bark from the tiger a good way away. I tried again, and bedad it responded again, nearer this time. I was excited Kate, and a bit nervous; the light was beginning to fade. I gave another softer bark and again the growly bark came back. I knew then that the tiger was at the other end of the path I was on. It was in the shadows and I had no chance of hitting it unless it came out into the open. I readied my rifle against my shoulder and gave, what was this time, just a nervous cough and didn't he come right out into the path. I took aim, fired, and hit him. He dropped and I moved closer and shot him again. I felt faint after that, and had to sit down for a few minutes. Well as you can imagine, I was a bit of a hero with the villagers and got a good price for the skin. It will make a magnificent snarling tiger rug for someone. I would have liked to have kept it but it would not have been practical."

Then unexpectedly, in the spring of 1866 Kate's father died of a heart attack. They had not long returned from a trip to the pier in Kingstown where he had enjoyed watching the yachts bobbing at rest, and the utter absorption of the children playing further out near Sandycove. Returning by rail, he commented on the lovely contours of Howth Head across the waters of the bay, but had been quiet as they walked slowly back to the house and was barely inside the door when he fell forward, dead. The doctor told her mother later that death had been instantaneous; a massive heart attack.

Nan looked after her mother while Kate and Elisa made all the arrangements. She could hardly remember what these were, she told Vincent, and indeed had little memory of anything during the days following his death. She did remember that he looked composed and serious in his silk lined coffin, and she could recall the hushed atmosphere of the dining room where he was laid out. The blinds were drawn and the wax candles and flowers gave off a heady but oppressive scent as the low murmuring of prayers continued through the long evening and night. There were the subdued sounds of condolences given and accepted in the drawing room where Nan and Lucy presided over refreshments, and where her mother sat very still, responding automatically to the words of sympathy being proffered. Dr Corbett helped the men to whiskey or porter.

Hardest for Kate were the condolences of the men and women who had worked closely with him over a period, in some cases, of more than thirty years, their sorrow and shock now exacerbated by the uncertainty that hung over their future. She remembered thinking slightly hysterically that Jimjo Tierney seemed so pale and shrunken, that her father's corpse looked almost healthy beside him, while poor Miss Edgeworth kept kneading her hands in what had felt like a mixture of anger and pain.

Kate left the house suddenly at about seven thirty and leant against the railings for a minute, she could hardly breathe. When she had recovered she made her way down to the river bemused by the ordinariness of life all around. The jarveys loitered as usual at Westland Row station, the harness of the patient horses clanking as they stamped their feet. She leant against the wall of the river watching the smoke curling skywards from the galleys of the ships and the water wrinkling in response to the breeze blowing over it, while the clamour of the Sunday bells awakened her to the finality of his death. It was her first taste of that profound loneliness which follows on the death of someone with whom one's life has been lovingly intertwined. It was a loneliness that she was to revisit many times over the course of her life.

The black crepe already attached to the door startled her on her return. She had not been missed and went straight to where her father was laid out and tried to pray. She remembered becoming distracted, and then enraged by the whisperings of Lucy and Miss O Neill: "He looks so peaceful and resigned, shure indeed he does, who'd have thought he'd make such a grand corpse, poor man, it will be a comfort to his family." She recalled that they looked hurt when she asked them to be quiet. The following day family and friends filled St Andrews church for the solemn requiem mass, after which Kate followed him on his final journey through the streets he knew so well to the cemetery. She remembered the light illuminating the polished oak and silver ornaments on the coffin as it was lowered into the grave. It seemed to bely the awful finality of that last handful of clay thrown on it before they moved away.

It was some weeks later that she wrote a full account of his death to John Jo, and to her great joy, in his reply he stated his intention of returning to Dublin and reiterating his hope that she would still want to marry him. Kate was both comforted and excited by this and also a little frightened.

Three months later she stood on the pier in Kingstown awaiting the boat that brought him back to her.

CHAPTER [4]

Marriage / children Decision to leave Dublin 1869-1884

"For this cause shall a man leave father and mother, and shall cleave to his wife: and they twain shall be one flesh."

Matthew Ch. 19 Vs. 5

Her first experience of the ceremony of "Religious Profession," was when Sister Gertrude took her vows of poverty, chastity and obedience as Kate led the choir in the beautiful *Veni Sponsa Christi.* Her own joy on receiving the black veil of her profession was of a different order to that of her marriage to John Jo.

KATE SMILED as she recalled her first walk in the park with John Jo a month or so after his return. She had recovered by then from her initial shyness. They had all been a little in awe of the lean, tanned and confident young man who had disembarked at Kingstown on that Tuesday morning in early December. "I suppose you fell in love with those beautiful Indian women," she had joked. "Oh yes," he said happily. "They are so beautiful and move with a shimmering grace and those liquid brown eyes - a man could drown in them." "Well," she said caustically, "I suppose there's safety in numbers." "I don't know about that," he said "Abdullah seemed to manage three, I think myself that four would be a good number," at which point Kate hit him and recalled him taking hold of both her hands: "You are a goose Kate," he said, pulling her into his arms to kiss her and with this she had to be satisfied.

It had not been so on that first morning of his return. She had been miserable, convinced that he would wonder how he could ever have cared for her. During the days that followed she avoided being alone with him until the Sunday when, after lunch he said to her mother, "Kate and I will take a walk in the park Mrs Corbett." She could still recall the rising panic which beset her. Inside the gate he had pulled her roughly to a standstill. "Kate have you decided that you don't want to marry me after all, is that what all this is about?" She had stared at him, astounded. "So you don't love me any more?" "No, yes" she had floundered. "So you think I don't love you any more?" Kate just stood there feeling so miserable and he looked so angry. "Listen Kate," he said "You have put me through hell these past few days; when I don't love you any more I will tell you so, loud and clear." Then his anger disappeared and she cried with relief as he stroked her head. It was a comfort to her to be able to tell Vincent that, in all the years they were together, he had never told her that he did not love her.

John Jo had saved enough money to purchase a modest house and understood from his old boss in the Registry of Deeds department, that he would be offered a post there if he applied, which he did. He had, he said, "enough of gallivanting around the world for a while, and the thought, Kate, of having you waiting for me in our own home of an evening, is something I have been looking forward to for a long time now." He held her close as he said this, and her cup of contentment was then very full.

Two more years were to elapse before their wedding day in September 1869. Kate could recall the day well. She was proud of how distinguished John Jo looked in his morning suit as he waited for her at the communion rail of St Andrews

Church. He was a little solemn and strained, though this eased when she smiled, and by the time the priest asked, "Do you take...." they were both peaceful and very sure in their responses. There was a moment of sadness at the memory of that last procession behind her father's coffin as they processed down the aisle, and a comforting squeeze of John Jo's hand. She remembered praying for the grace to make God's love real in their marriage.

Then all was a blur of congratulations and toasts; the tinkling of glasses and cups and saucers, a barrage of rice and good wishes, tearful hugs from Elisa and her mother, and finally the cab whisking them to Kingstown station and the train for Galway. As she collapsed into her seat she raised the little veil from her face, and caught a reflection of the lime green silk of her blouse shimmering in the mirror, adding a touch of gaiety to her navy blue linen suit.

Tired out by the emotion and the excitement of the day, they were both quiet on the journey. They were to spend three nights in the splendid Great Southern Hotel and then on to a remote little hotel in Connemara, recommended by a colleague of John Jo's, a fishing enthusiast who had persuaded him that it was much to be preferred to Killarney, the more usual destination for newly weds. By the time they arrived in Galway, the lamp-lighters were out and Kate recalled the delicious smell of roast potatoes floating up from a hawker's fire glowing on the kerb as they made their way to the hotel.

It had been a long time coming, more than eight years since they first met. Kate was twenty one then and John Jo just twenty. Now they were alone together, bound for their remaining days "for better or for worse" and were wonderfully strange to each other. The pleasure of those early days of married love was intoxicating and indeed all-consuming for a time. Kate often thought it one of the Good Lord's more quixotic blessings, this strange tenderness that can forge such a firm union between quite disparate sorts of beings. John Jo always held a certain mystery for her, and she never really understood his emotional or reflective life, though paradoxically, she felt that she knew him more fully than he knew himself. She did not know if it was the same for him as it was not something they discussed.

They walked the claddagh by sunset and paddled in the sea at Salthill, storing up images that would last their lifetime. Then, rested and invigorated, they set off by coach for Roundstone, and thence by cab to their hotel. It was a lovely welcoming place with a warm fire burning in the sitting room. Kate loved the quiet of the blue and purple mountains, and the reed grown lakes alive with birdsong. They tramped through a landscape where the mood and hues of mountain, lake and bog land were transformed as the constantly changing weather dictated. A light, sun-filled landscape would give way to ominous high winds, lashing rain and glowering hilltops with little warning.

It was on one such day when they set out in bright sunshine on a lovely mossy track through an area of extensive bogland that the skies suddenly changed and unleashed their fury. Within a short space of time it seemed as if they inhabited a universe consisting entirely of water. It was all around them in lakes and rivers; it cascaded from the skies, poured down their faces, and it felt as if their very bones might be made of the stuff.

"Come on Kate let's run." John Jo took her hand, and after what seemed an eternity, they came out on to a road, where they saw a light glowing in a small longish cottage. It was a public house and grocer shop. There was a smoky lamp hanging from the ceiling, casting a low shadowy light, and a turf fire against the gable wall with an old man sitting by it, and two other men leaning against the counter talking to the proprietor. Kate was puzzled for a while, unable to make out what they were saying, then realised that they were speaking in Gaelic. They stopped courteously as they entered and the old man insisted on her taking his chair by the fire. The proprietor asked John Jo if she would like a cup of tea and Kate nodded gratefully. They must have been there for about two hours waiting

for the rain to clear. There was a fiddle hanging on the wall and
John Jo asked if anyone played; one of the men leaning against
the counter took it down and played some jigs and a very long
melancholic air that the company seemed to appreciate, as they
kept patting him on the back encouragingly and murmuring
"maith an fear" which she gathered meant "good man". Then
they offered it to Kate but she passed it to John Jo who could
play a little. He played the *Londonderry Air* and followed it
up with some jigs and his dancing accompaniment, to their
great delight.

Kate relished the memory of the fun and good humour of
this occasion, but could never tell her mother, or indeed many
of their friends about it, for it would have been shocking to
them for a lady of any refinement to enter such premises. But
indeed, as she said, nothing could have surpassed the kindness
of those men, and the innocent fun of the occasion should not
give offence to anyone of sense.

On the return journey to Dublin they spent some time in
Ballagh at the home of John Jo's brother Tom and his wife Ellen
in Clare, and this was Kate's first visit to the lovely house
Vincent was to grow up in, and would one day inherit. Little
did she know when they enjoyed their light hearted visit that
they, and Ballagh, were to become such a significant part of her
own family life. Tom and John Jo spent their time fishing
and shooting, while Ellen and Kate discussed furnishings and
other domestic matters of interest to them both. The shadow of
Ellen's childlessness was still in the future and they had a very
happy time together.

The following decade when all of her six beloved children
were born, was one of great contentment for Kate. They lived
initially in the lovely old village of Blackrock very near the
sea where the three eldest boys were born. She loved being
mistress of her own establishment, and took pride in caring
for it with the help of Maria her housemaid. Maria had been
one of the orphans cared for by the Sisters of Mercy in Baggot street and Kate got to know and value her there. She

could recall delighting especially in the glowing polished surfaces of the furniture, particularly the lovely inlaid bureau made for them by her father's old cabinet maker Jimjo Tierney and the cunningly wrought mahogany writing box with its' secret drawers - the only piece she was to bring with her to the New World years later.

John Jo too loved to return to the welcome of his home in those early days, and together they wondered at the mystery of the emerging characters of their children and laughed at their antics. Mind you, it was very hard work then, with continuous washing cooking and cleaning, and though Kate was fortunate in having a good laundry service nearby which took care of the bed linen and John Jo's shirts, there was still much to do. The days passed in a blur of housework, caring, soothing upsets and tantrums, tiredness and contentment.

She had so many vivid images from their lives then – the rush of air in the hallway at around 6 o'clock, "How is my Kate and her brood?" … the boys jostling each other to be first to reach him. He would swing the first to arrive up on his shoulder and the next two got a hand each while he made his way to the sitting room and listened with interest to the doings of the day.

After dinner they would sometimes read or chat, and enjoyed making music together or with friends. John Jo had a great interest in the music of his own country which many regarded as of little worth. He would spend hours with his fiddle, learning tunes out of the vast volume collected by Edward Bunting which Kate would play along with on the piano. She did not share his passion for these, and indeed he was not a great musician, but she loved his enthusiasm. He conveyed so well the feeling of a song, and for some reason, it was those of the Scottish poet Robert Burns, that she remembered most vividly, and most particularly *Ae Fond Kiss* which he loved to sing, and did so beautifully.

She looked back with gratitude on that first year of their married life as one of great tenderness and some excitement.

She would catch John Jo watching her as she removed the globe to trim the wick of the lamp in their little sitting room, or as she loosed her hair in the mirror of their dressing table before retiring, and an answering tenderness would well up within her. They held each other close against the uncertainty of the future.

The focus of their lives changed as the children arrived and they became fully absorbed by them. There was a lot of fun: "Come on boys," John Jo would say on Saturday afternoons and all would head down to Sandymount beach, while Maria and Kate followed with a picnic. When the tide was out they were just specks in the distance. Then the vast stretches of sand, sea and sky, encircled by the lovely hills of Dublin and Wicklow, held them in their magic embrace. There were many outings over the years that followed, to hill and seaside as well as visits to friends and family.

They had moved to a larger house in 11 Careysfort Avenue by the time Edie was born in 1874, and they were pleased to have their first little girl. Kate was very tired and knew that John Jo was becoming anxious as it was not five years since they had married and already they had four children. They had taken a cab out to Milltown shortly after Edie's birth to go for a walk along one of their favourite haunts by the Dodder. John Jo was troubled, "Kate I am sorry" he said "you look so weary, you re exhausted from all the pregnancies and you re only thirty three." "I will try to be more careful," he continued, "but it's your own fault for being so irresistible." They laughed and she took his face in her hands and assured him of her contentment. He did not say any more then, but they did not have another child until Kath was born in 1877 and finally Vincent in 1879. By then they had moved to Glasnevin where they were to remain until they sailed for New York in 1884.

The emergence of all their children's characters was of abiding interest to John Jo and Kate during those years and indeed the truism that, "the child is father to the man" seemed in retrospect very apparent. Pat's love of music and perform-ance, which his brothers called 'showing off', became appar-ent. He taught himself fiddle, and he and John Jo spent hours together playing tunes from Bunting's. Kate was glad of the bond it created between them. One of the few crises she re-membered from those early years related to an incident when Pat took a flute from a boy in his school. The following evening the boy's father came to the door and told them that Pat had stolen his boy's flute. She recalled so well Pat's pale face, frightened by the unaccustomed sternness of his father as he asked if he had taken the flute. He stuttered as he always did when upset and could not get any words out. He turned around and left the room returning a minute or so later with the flute. John Jo apologised to the parent and assured him that this would not happen again, and that he would deal with it. When he left John Jo took the cane from where it was kept behind the door, but until then, never used, and told Pat to go to his room where he would see him in a minute. Kate could not bear this; she knew that the child had no malice in him and while alarmed, was clearly bemused by the anger con-verging on him. To John Jo's horror she began to cry and this escalated into rather hysterical sobbing. "Kate what is the matter? It's not such an awful thing – it happens with lots of children and it won't happen again. I'll give him a good beat-ing he'll remember." This of course made her worse: "No, no – you can't do that."

Kate smiled as she recalled John Jo's completely bewildered and indeed alarmed expression. When she had quietened down she explained that Pat did not know that he had done wrong, and that they needed to explain to him why everyone was angry. John Jo was still doubtful but too worried about her to risk any further upset, and indeed, when they asked Pat why he had taken it, he said, "Thomas never played it and when I asked him if I could, he said I could keep it if I liked. It is so easy Kate told Vincent, to do an injustice to a little child. She prayed that God would keep him always from any word or act that might harm one of His little ones.

Jack and Louis were both keen on sports and joined the junior athletics association run by the local branch of the Temperance movement, where Louis in particular shone. Even as a child, Jack had a calm, even temperament and a good practical intelligence that he applied to anything he turned his hand to. Louis' interest was always in the moment, and his competitive spirit throve on sports. Edie's imaginative and contented personality was a particular delight to Kate as she made a wonderful little companion. Kath brought with her an enlivening injection of high-spirited energy, while Vincent was a contented, self-contained and hugely loved child.

The latter part of the 1870s and the early 1880s were not easy for John Jo. He was still young and energetic and his office life had become increasingly tedious and enervating. There was little or no challenge for someone of his abilities and opportunities for promotion were rare, as members of the ascendancy class were still the preferred candidates for the more senior governmental posts. There was a great upsurge in political life in the city and indeed throughout the country during those years under the leadership of Parnell, and to this John Jo increasingly devoted his interest and his time. He would meet with like minded friends in taverns throughout the city, and relished the sense of purpose and comradeship they provided. Kate was fearful that they would get him into trouble with the police or his employers, for he was very outspoken. She also worried about his drinking, which escalated during this period. She had hoped that Vincent's arrival might alter his habit of staying out increasingly late, but this had not happened.

She remembered one occasion from that period when she had kept dinner back in the hope that he would arrive in time, but it was after 9:30 when he came home. "I had some veal cutlets and very good lamb in the Griffin," he said in response to her offer of food. "John Jo what are we going to do?" Kate said. "You spend most evenings out. We need you and we also cannot afford to waste money, we have six children to provide for." She could recall the wry smile with which he replied "Its always 'the children' Kate, you don't need me, you have everything you want," and added, "I spend my days shuffling around that poky room, copying out documents that any of our boys could do now, with no prospects. I need to breathe sometimes, and I believe I can make a contribution to improving the conditions in our country which affect our children's future. I do enjoy meeting up with my friends, we have a bit of fun and I can have a decent conversation."

Kate was quiet, startled by the tinge of bitterness, and obscurely chastised by a sense of the justice of his words, for she had not given much thought to his circumstances and he rarely complained. Neither could she refute his charge that she had everything she needed, because, while of course she loved him and always would, she no longer had that urgent need of him that had characterised their early married life. He was aware of this, and felt diminished by its absence. He did try to come home earlier after that, but his heart was not in it, and the old closeness was gone. He seemed listless and no longer initiated Saturday outings or played with the children.

On one or two occasions in the past John Jo had spoken about the opportunities for advancement available in America, where he had a number of friends and two cousins all doing well. At the time Kate had not paid much heed; the boys were well settled into their school in Blackrock and were doing well under the guidance of the Holy Ghost fathers there. Edie too was thriving at school under the imaginative teaching of Sister Vincent, a gentle Dominican nun, and Kath was due to join her there shortly. In addition, life for Kate was very pleasant, surrounded as she was by family and friends.

However following John Jo's outburst, the seed planted by these earlier comments began to take root, and she started to gather information about America and more specifically New York State, and the prospects there for a growing family.

There was a lot of information available then, as nearly every family they knew had friends or relatives living there, and all seemingly doing well. One of John Jo's cousins had a management position in a big company that sold farm equipment. He had emigrated in the late 1860s, shortly after John Jo's return from India, and had been very insistent about the excellent prospects there, for educated men of farming background. Kate had always been aware that it was only John Jo's domestic responsibilities that held him back from trying his luck there.

About a year or so later they set out for what was to be a memorable family picnic. It was late August, and there was an aura of adventure about the occasion. The picnic basket, fishing rods, hurling sticks and jam jars had all been packed the night before, and all were up early to catch the coach to Roundwood. There, they bought gingerbread biscuits and lemonade for the children while the horses were changed, and then on through the lovely hilly scenery past Luggelaw and into Blessington, before the final stretch to the river and wonderful falls at Poulaphouca. It was a blessed day, the sun shone and John Jo joined the boys and Kath in an energetic game of hurling before taking Edie upstream with him to teach her to fish. The others played in the river, splashing each other and hunting for minnows until it was time to eat. The slices of cold chicken and ham, the tomatoes, hard boiled eggs, scallions and the buttered brown soda bread all disappeared in a flash as did every crumb of the special plum cake Maria had baked for the occasion.

It was on the return journey when the children were dozing off in the coach, that Kate said, "John Jo, I think we should consider emigration to New York." She recalled him looking at her unbelievingly. "You are joking Kate?" She assured him that she was serious. "But you love Dublin, you would hate to leave it, and the children are settled and there's your mother and sister." "I know," she said "I have been thinking about it for nearly a year now and I think I will find it hard but I believe we should try it." "Why?" he asked bluntly. "Neither of us is getting younger and what if it didn't work out?" "It might not" she said, "and we'll have to cross that bridge if it happens, but I am confident that you will rise to the challenge and make the most of the opportunities like you did in India. You are suffocating in your job here and it makes you unhappy which affects us all. But it's not only you, I am also thinking of our boys. We will have little to leave them and their prospects are limited in Ireland."

John Jo gave her a warm hug then, which was she felt, gratitude enough for what had been a proposal she had come to slowly and with a lot of heartache. The next year was one of preparation and planning. Hardest of all was telling her mother, then, in her early seventies and Elisa to whom she was very close. "I think it is the right decision Kate," her mother said "Your children's prospects there are likely to be considerably better than here," and she cried a little, and indeed Kate cried a lot more as she patted her shoulder comfortingly. "You'll be back to visit; people are coming back every three or four years now." For Elisa it was particularly hard, as they depended on each other in so many ways and Kate would be leaving her with sole responsibility for their mother's care.

It was agreed that her mother and Elisa would purchase their house as plans were already in place to sell the family business and they would use the money to get settled in New York. The older boys would remain with Kate's mother and Elisa, continuing at school until Kate and John Jo had found somewhere to live, when they would join them. There was uproar from the boys at this but Kate and John Jo were adamant.

It was wonderful for her to see John Jo's spirit and vigour renewed. Following correspondence with his cousin he secured a position as salesman for farm machinery in upstate New York. She recalled with great joy those evenings when they sat around the sitting room table while he read to them about life in New York and other parts of the United States; the soft glow from the lamp lit up the circle of excited faces cupped in little elbows, the velvet table cloth shimmered in the light, and the different hues of each head of hair were burnished by its rays. Then, Kate would feel that the price for such zest and enthusiasm was low, but there were very many times when the prospect of the uprooting to be faced seemed too much to bear. Everything around her became unbearably precious. The sights and sounds of her childhood were everywhere - beautiful St Stephen's Green, Sandymount strand, the ducks and moorhens on the canal, the banter of the cabmen and street hawkers, the elegiac lamplighters and the beauty of the blossom on that last summer before they left.

Of especial poignancy was their final outing to Glendalough. There, under cloudless skies, this magical valley taunted her with its haunting beauty. The children except for Pat ran ahead toward the round tower as they entered the ruined monastic city, and they could glimpse the lough beyond. Pat was entranced and listened avidly to John Jo's account of monastic Ireland, the broken symbols of which lay all around them. He pointed out St Kieran's Church, St Kevin's well and a lovely Celtic cross. He spoke of the tonsured monks chanting from illuminated manuscripts by the light of tallow candles, sending out a beacon of light and learning throughout Europe.

She remembered how Pat delighted particularly in the miracles attributed to St Kevin - the pathos of his instruction to a deer, "that it shed its milk each day to provide nourishment for a baby whose mother died in childbirth" – the story of the bird that laid its eggs in his cupped palms, requiring him to maintain them in this position until the chicks hatched and were reared. "Of course Pat" said John Jo, "he really knew how to manage women because you know they can be a great nuisance," and he pointed to a rocky ledge over the lake. "You see that Pat, that's St Kevin's bed, and he had to make it up there to stop the women chasing him, and even so didn't one of them climb up after him." "What did he do Dad?" said Pat "Oh he pushed her into the lake, sure what else could he do the poor man." Pat looked shocked but this quickly turned to glee as Kate and Elisa beat John Jo with their gloves and chased him along the path.

When they got to the lakeside Kate looked back at the round tower wrought by the hands of faith a thousand years before. There was no cloud in the sky or stir in the reeds at the edge of the lough behind her. She thought to herself, "There were probably days like this when they were building that tower, and there will be days like this to enshrine its beauty and holiness in the years to come but I won't see them." She felt then, she told Vincent, as if she might die of sadness, and walked quickly away and back towards the entrance, as she did not want to spoil the day with her tears and was glad that they had not been noticed.

The final weeks passed in a frenzy of preparation, packing, goodbyes, abjurations and promises to write. When she said goodbye to her mother Kate did not know that she would never see her again, nor indeed, as they stepped onto the sleek steamship the *Celtic,* that she was about to embark upon a journey of crucifying pain and loss, but one for which she would eventually be grateful.

CHAPTER 5

The voyage – Kate's calvary
Upper NY State 1884-1886

"Thou shalt break them with a rod of iron; thou shalt dash them in pieces like a potter's vessel."

Psalm 2 Vs. 9

The little cloister garden, which Kate could see from the infirmary window looked damp and dreary, reflecting the aridity of her efforts to pray and reminding her of those painful years after she left Ireland. She was thankful for the faith that allowed her to bear this cross with equanimity now. It had not been so then.

KATE'S EARLIEST memory of the voyage had been Vincent's voice. "Mam, Mam, it's a whale. It's huge, nearly the size of the ship." He ran across the deck towards her, his little face alight with excitement. "It is Kate, a bull I think, by the size of it." John Jo arrived in his wake almost as elated. They joined the crowd gathered at the starboard, and watched the immense sleek creature slide to the surface. It frothed water from its huge jaws before insinuating itself back into the depths with such a sense of restrained power.

Only two days at sea and already their life on board ship had drawn them into its own concerns. Its immediacy absorbed them and relegated past and future lives to dreamier realms. They embarked on a bright but chilly September morning, and remained on deck to watch Queenstown gradually fade from view. Kate remembered the steeple of its cathedral caught in the sun's rays, flashing them a final salute.

Those first days were ones of great excitement for the children and hardly less so for John Jo, released from the bondage of the narrow world of the Registry of Deeds office. They set about exploring their new environment and soon made friends among the passengers and crew. Kate found herself infected with an exhilarating sense of expectancy, caught up not only in her own hopes and apprehensions but in those of their fellow passengers.

She was strolling on the promenade deck one evening with Cornelius Murphy, a rather floridly dressed but nonetheless respectable man of about forty five. He had one of those pleasingly irregular faces with a jutting chin and very firm expression, and she and John Jo had grown to like him. They made their way to the forecastle where they could hear the sounds of fiddle and concertina, and came upon a very merry scene indeed. There, amongst dozens of people from steerage were John Jo and the children, dancing with great energy and abandon what, she believed, was known as the *Clare set*. John Jo loved to dance and relished the intricate dance music passed down through generations of players. He had met the three Delaney boys from Clare whose father had been known to him as a child, when boarding the ship, and they had invited them to join in the dancing. It was beautiful to watch as the ordered complexity of the steps contrasted with the wilder twirling and stamping of the larger group.

Kate mentioned to Cornelius that she thought some of the people looked very poor and undernourished, and he turned to her astonished: "It's easily known, Kate, that you have not seen real hunger. When I left Ireland as a lad of fifteen some thirty years ago, I was one of hundreds half dead from starvation. There were men and women sick and dying packed like sardines alongside the healthy in the bowels of the ship with every kind of vermin you could imagine. There were rats, mice, cockroaches, and everywhere you looked there was death. Every day one, two sometimes five bodies would be taken away and buried at sea. But it was the stench I remember most. There were only two water closets and these were often blocked. The reek of vomit, of rotting and rotten food, of stale sweat and diarrhoea, mildewed blankets and rotgut poitín ...you could never get away from it, and eventually you learnt to live with the fact that you were part of it. I vowed then, that if I ever made it to New York I would work every daylight hour to get away from that smell. I spent seven years working on the building sites of New York's tenements and railways, and then I set myself up as a building contractor in my own right and I've never looked back. Most of the people I left Ireland with were already worn out and without hope. These people" he continued, pointing to the wild dancers, "have hope, they'll make something of their lives." Kate found his words heartening and felt them to be a good omen for their future.

The weather was clear and warm during those first days, and the ship, cushioned by a gentle sea was borne agreeably over its calm undulating surface. The sense of isolation and unaccustomed leisure had a narcotic effect on John Jo and Kate as they moved pleasurably between their cabin, the grand saloon and the promenade deck. Peggy Moran, an energetic and rather shy young girl from a large Tipperary farming family took charge of Kath and Edie to their great delight. She was being brought out to New York by her uncle, a parish priest there, who would educate her and find her suitable employment. Kate admired her courage as she battled her loneliness and fears and was, she felt, glad of the distraction involved in caring for her little girls. The three Delaney boys took Vincent in tow and he had a wonderful time, learning to dance and play the concertina when not riding around on their shoulders. It was a time of recuperation for them both after the tiring months of preparation and anxiety, and they were very happy, and curiously indifferent to the uncertainty that lay before them.

This all changed on the fifth day. The wind began to whip up in the morning and by mid afternoon the sky was black. The sea, charcoal-coloured and suddenly ominous, was heaving violently and their solid ship was transformed into a piece of helpless driftwood. Everywhere there were people being sick and the decks were streaked with vomit. Kate and Vincent became violently ill, and the child kept begging her to stop the ship! She remembered trying to hold the bucket for him but needing to be sick herself: he, poor child, knocked it over and the floor was covered in the bile-like stuff. John Jo had to clean it up for them as all the stewards were fully occupied. He took Kath and Edie up on deck, holding on to them tightly, as he held this to be the best way of avoiding seasickness, and indeed neither he nor they succumbed. It was a miserable twenty four hours before the storm played itself out, and then they both recovered just as suddenly as they had become ill. Again the sea was gentle and playful, as though that surge of rage and power had never been.

They were only five days away from New York when Kath became ill. She was listless and tired and would eat little. When, a couple of days later she remained fatigued, and began to complain of a sore throat and of difficulty in swallowing, they became concerned. Kath had always been a robust child who liked her food, and tended to throw off infections easily. Kate consulted her *Practical Home Physician*, and it was here that she was first confronted with the possibility that it might be diphtheria. She asked John Jo to get Dr Ferguson, the ship's physician, to come and examine Kath. This was a dreaded disease and she knew it was infectious but did not then allow herself to dwell on the fact that Edie and Kath had shared a bed in their cabin since embarkation. She initially believed that her symptoms were those of a minor infection, and because of this was not unduly anxious. However she did make up a bed for Edie in their cabin, explaining to the bewildered child that Kath was ill and needed to be quiet and on her own.

Kate had just finished praying the angelus with her at midday when Kath told her that she needed to go the toilet. It was then, as she began to wrap a warm blanket around her that Kath slid to the floor in a faint from which she never recovered consciousness. By the time John Jo arrived with Dr Ferguson Kath was in a deep coma, and by six o'clock that evening she was dead. He confirmed that she had died of diphtheria, which must, he said, have been transmitted by one of her playfellows. He told them that there had been a number of cases in the midlands of England and that there were fears of an epidemic there, and of course their boat had taken on English emigrants in Liverpool.

Dr Ferguson was normally a quiet rather acerbic man who wasted neither words nor time and had himself embarked at Liverpool. Originally from Montrose in Scotland, he was, a little distrustful of women, though Kate thought that it may have been shyness, and she remembered with gratitude his kindness then. He arranged for Sister Agnes, one of two Sisters of Charity on board who were going out to join their Sisters in caring for the sick in St Vincent's Hospital in New York, to supervise the disinfecting of cabin and clothes and to prepare her little girl's body for the last rites of the Church.

Kate was in shock; it had all happened so quickly. She remembered nothing of the requiem Mass said by young Father Quigley, but the image of that small shape encased in a canvas sheet and weighted down with a stone, remained with her all her life. It was when they got ready to commit her little body to the sea ... that little body she had cushioned with her own ... that she cried out. She was distraught with anguish and hardly rational. She recalled, "I wanted to go with it until it was safe in the arms of Our Blessed Mother in Heaven," and fell on her knees praying, "Oh dear Lord, do not let our little girl be engulfed by those fearsome depths." John Jo dropped on his knees to hold her, his own face rigid with pain. Then the child was gone.

Kate prayed as she recounted her story, that the good God would never see fit to lay such a heavy cross on Vincent's shoulders, though she added, that it was only by his Grace that she had learnt to bear it.

She did not need to be told that Edie was in great danger of contracting the disease because of her constant proximity to Kath. She could not grieve for Kath then, but had to focus all her energy on Edie and Vincent. With tact and real kindness, Dr Ferguson arranged for the ingredients required for treatment to be brought to her by Sister Agnes. This kindly nun patiently explained what to do, should either of the children become ill, going over the instructions with John Jo because she realised that Kate was in no fit state to take them in. The day before they arrived in New York, Edie began to show some of the early signs of the contagion. She lost her appetite and became listless with a slight fever. Then they were in New York, surrounded by the huge noise of immigration and disembarkation procedures.

Kate remembered little of how arrangements were made, but learnt afterwards that it was Dr Ferguson and Sister Agnes in consultation with the medical officials from the Immigration Department who negotiated their transfer to the home of a remarkable Quaker lady called Lisa Rice, who lived near St Vincent's hospital in West 11th street. She was a childless widow who had become a good friend to the Sisters of Charity whose work in the hospital she greatly admired. Her simply furnished home was almost spartan. There were no coverings on the bare floorboards, and the walls were painted in plain pale shades. The furniture was simple and functional and everywhere was spotlessly clean. Kate would never forget the selfless kindness of this truly Christian woman who shared the nursing of Edie and the care of Vincent during those tormented days.

For the first day or so she clung to the hope that it was Edie's confusion and grief over Kath's death that was responsible. By the third day when she began to complain of a sore throat and Kate could see some swelling there and the little tell-tale white spots, she knew that she had succumbed. For three further days she coaxed her to swallow the half teaspoon of brandy mixed with a quarter grain of quinine prescribed by Dr Ferguson, and used the little camel-hair brush Sister Agnes had brought her, to apply the recommended solution of glycerine, hyposulphite and water, directly to Edie's poor sore little throat. It was pitiable to see the effort it cost her to swallow even a few drops of water, but hardest of all during those three days were the child's confused and sometimes frightened questions – "Will I die like Kath?... where is Kath now? ... will I go to heaven too? ... what is heaven like?"

Exhausted and numbed with sorrow and dread, Kate could not pray. How could she say "Thy Will be Done?" She had just lost one of her little girls. Though she asked forgiveness later for her lapse of faith, and knew that the Good Lord who forgave Peter three times would have no difficulty forgiving her, it seemed beyond her strength then.

It was John Jo who came to her aid. He who had rarely evinced any great conviction of faith was able so simply to evoke such a sense of joy for Edie. He stroked her hair gently and asked her, "Do you remember our picnic at Poulaphouca in the summer?" and when she nodded, went on to call to mind that magical day. "You remember you had to hold Vincent's hand by the waterfall because he was a little frightened, and you sat on my lap when I showed you how to hold the fishing rod and what a fright you got when we caught that little trout?" A half smile played around Edie's lips as John Jo vividly recalled the happy images. She drifted into unconsciousness before he was able to make any comforting links to her questions about heaven, and she died that night. Kate liked to think that the images he evoked gave her some sense of the joy that was to come, and that she died in peace.

Kate wept then, as if her heart would break and indeed she felt that it had. She wept for Kath for whom she had neither grieved nor prayed because of her fierce focus on Edie. She wept for what she felt to be her lost life. She raged at the Lord:

"Why let my little girls be born if it was just to destroy them and they hungry for life?" Kate wept for hours, and John Jo, 'God be good to him', held her for hours.

She could remember little of the simple ceremony which took place in the chapel of St Vincent's hospital. All the arrangements were made by Sister Agnes and Mrs Rice. Edie was buried in a small plot in Mount Olivet, the purchase of which was arranged by Cornelius Murphy. Those good people who were no kin to them were, Kate told Vincent, "shining vessels of God's care of us in our anguish." It was to be many months before she could write to express her gratitude to them, but never a day went by that she failed to remember them in her prayers. Edie's little grave was marked by two crosses to commemorate both Kath and herself.

Kate could not say how they picked themselves up and journeyed on to Buffalo. She did know that they were again assisted greatly by Cornelius Murphy, and that they moved into a house John Jo's cousin had rented for them in the respectable west side. John Jo decided to send for the older boys sooner than they had planned, believing that the demands of caring for all of them would help Kate over her grief.

Those early months in America remained hazy in her memory. She told Vincent that he had missed his sisters greatly at first, and that it was his continual questioning that helped her to grieve. "Will the whale have eaten Kath? ... Will they meet each other in heaven? ... Will you and Dad die? ..." and so on, each question a fresh wound; but she thanked God that she was able to reassure him and in so doing began to heal herself.

She registered him in the local parish school and her fears that he might find it difficult to settle proved groundless. He quickly made friends with a little boy whose name, she remembered, was Barney Driscoll. She found it an ease as did John Jo to see Vincent gradually resume an absorption in his own childhood world.

Then came the day in early November when John Jo said, "Well Vin, I think you and I should take a holiday tomorrow,

what do you think about a jaunt to New York on the train?"
His little face alight, he asked, "Can we go to the zoo Dad?"
"We'll see what we have time for," John Jo had replied. Kate
would love to have seen Vincent's expression when he saw Pat,
Jack and Louis waving from the boat whilst waiting to disem-
bark. John Jo told her later that Vincent tore his hand from his
and went racing across the wharves to meet them and Jack
scooped him up on to his shoulders.

There were tears in both of their eyes as they thought of the
absence of Kath and Edie at that welcome. John Jo told them
very simply about their deaths, and all five of them went to
Mount Olivet and laid flowers on the little grave that commem-
orated both. Pat was particularly distressed and Vincent tried
to comfort him, telling him about heaven.

The older boys settled into the routine at Canisius High
School run by the Jesuits, and they were very fortunate in that
the parish to which they belonged was very active both socially
and spiritually. Louis and Jack proved adept at baseball, thereby
securing a solid niche for themselves both in school and in the
parish, which was very proud of its prowess at baseball. Pat not
only joined the school choir but quickly became a leading light
in the musical and dramatic life of the parish, in demand not
only as a singer, but also as an accompanist on the piano. It was
here too that his flair for acting came to light and was nurtured.

Most clearly etched on Kate's mind was the interior of St
Joseph's Cathedral, built by the labour, finance and above all
the Faith of the Irish immigrants. There, in its shadowed seren-
ity, lit only by the jewelled shafts of sunlight filtering through
the lovely Rose windows and the ruby and sapphire glints from
the vigil lights by the altar of the Blessed Virgin, she spent so
much of those first months. Peace did not come easily or
quickly, and she passed many a bleak hour hiding in that
church, unable to pray. Nevertheless she believed that our Lord
accepted her presence as itself a prayer, because it is to this
period that she traced the beginning of her real detachment
from earthly passions and loves.

She later looked back with great compassion on the loneliness of John Jo during this time. He never interfered with her religious life knowing how much in need of it she was. However he did not then have the kind of faith that would have allowed him recourse to its consolations, and she had not been sensitive to his struggle. She was not happy with the amount of time he spent in Jim Maloney's saloon bar, but in retrospect was aware that her increasing involvement in the life of the church left him to endure his loneliness in isolation, and that she must bear some responsibility for the fact that he turned to Maloney's for solace. She believed that God would forgive, as she did, his too great reliance on the comfort he found there.

Kate recalled John Jo's unfailing kindness to her during those difficult times, when the charity he showed her was, she believed, greater than she was able to offer him. She was very aware that the hours she spent in church were a search for consolation and not a mark of any great holiness. Indeed, she looked back with shame at how little of Our Lord's love and compassion she had been able to impart to some of those he entrusted to her care at that time.

It was with particular remorse that she thought of Brigid Moran, the young Limerick girl who came to work for them as a maid. She was a country girl with little experience of any refinement and Kate was less than patient in trying to teach her the basics of good housekeeping. She prayed now, she said, for forgiveness for the indifference bordering, at times, on cruelty, with which she regarded this poor girl. She could recall one particular occasion arriving in the kitchen, to see her turning from the range, which she had been cleaning, to cut Vincent a slice of soda bread with blackened hands. "What a dirty thing to do Brigid," Kate said with unpardonable cruelty, and the poor girl, as always, reddened at her words. John Jo whom she had not noticed, overheard and asked to speak with her. He closed the door of the sitting room carefully and turned to her white with anger. "For God's sake Kate," he said

"I never thought to see my wife, the mother of my children, inflict such cruelty on a fellow creature with even more to bear than we have. That girl is little more than a child, she has no family here and has had to leave everything she has known to try and make her way. It's little welcome she'll get from the folk here, but to think that we, who should know better, cannot offer her a bit of Christian kindness is cruel indeed." He walked out making no effort to soften the impact of his chastisement. Kate did not like the mirror he held up to her behaviour but it brought her to her senses. Brigid remained wary of her and Kate struggled with feelings of distaste from time to time, but she was never again guilty of cruelty or deliberate unkindness.

She recalled that it was on Palm Sunday that John Jo first mentioned the idea of "homesteading" to her. They were returning from the cathedral and she was still immersed in the grandeur and mystery of the procession and ceremonies. The music by Bach and Verdi had been given glorious voice by the massed male and female choirs and the haunting strains of a Handel oratorio taken up by solo violin was still percolating through her senses. She did not pay much attention at first as they greeted neighbours and fellow parishioners, but when he took her by the elbow and led her towards the quiet shaded aisle of fashionable Delaware Avenue with its magnificent overarching elms, she could see that he needed her attention.

It was not John Jo's way to labour his hardships but he spoke to her then about his experiences over the six or seven months that had elapsed since their arrival. She was truly shocked by the picture of prejudice, opposition and outright hostility to Irish Catholics which emerged. He gave examples of numerous humiliating incidents, all the more poignant for being relayed with his characteristic self deprecating humour. "I don't believe Kate," he said, "that we'll ever get on here. If anything the prejudice is worse than at home, and I fear for our boys' future." So cocooned had she been in the world of home and their supportive parish, that she had not noticed until then, the corrosive impact of this experience on John Jo. She was ashamed and cried a little for his courage and his humour, but he was undaunted and comforted her "We'll not be beaten, Kate," he said, patting her shoulder. He then went on to remind her about the homesteading legislation that would allow them to file for land, virtually free of charge, except for an initial small fee. "There are a number of men who meet regularly in Maloney's saloon planning to move west," he said, "and many have already done so. Business, banks and services follow, many owned or worked by Irish people, and – best of all, Kate - a land largely free of the stultifying ignorance and prejudice that surrounds us here."

Kate could not pretend that she found it easy to be enthusiastic at the thought of uprooting yet again. It had been so unexpected to find such a rich spiritual life in the parish of their new home and she had come to rely on the solace she found there. The thought of setting out for regions, still so wild and little known, filled her with dread. In addition, their parish was the centre of a well organised and stimulating social and cultural life from which all benefited. The boys had all made friends, playing cards and pool in the parish centre when not involved in baseball. Pat in particular was thriving on the recognition of, and support for his dramatic and musical talent, and all appreciated the astonishingly rich musical life of the parish. John Jo and Kate also enjoyed the lectures and recitals that were a regular feature of parish life. It was hard for her to leave all this, and indeed it was the pull and comfort of such supports that kept many of their acquaintances from braving the challenges of going west, where such comforts would be minimal for some time to come.

However, her soul, as she said, was strengthening a little with the help of her life of prayer, and by God's grace she was able to convey some measure of glad support to John Jo in his thinking and planning. She admired his courage and was determined not to fail him, and they were both committed to securing the best future they could for all of their boys. John

Jo was not deceived about the effort that this cost her and his gratitude brought a comforting return of closeness to them.

He began to correspond with officials and land registration offices, and though initially favouring Montana, he finally settled on Wyoming as their place of destination. There, he found an excellent site at the foot of Mt. Casper beside Elkhorn creek where there was an abundance of trees for firewood and building, and a healthy supply of water from the creek. This would be essential for irrigation purposes, and in addition contained plentiful supplies of trout.

As he began to make plans they talked to the boys about the move and the excitement grew. Louis, as always, embraced novelty and for Jack, this had ever been his dream - to head for the "wild west". Vincent always took his cue from Jack, so he too was happy. Pat said little, but Kate knew it was hard for him and watched, troubled, as he withdrew a little further into himself. He was not one to make a noise about his wishes but he had been thriving in his new milieu finding a recognition and support for his talents that was new for him. She feared that his essentially happy soul would shrivel for want of sustenance where they were going, and made a special novena to Our Blessed Mother asking her to make him her special care.

They had hoped that Joan and Steve McElligot with whom they had become friendly, and who were of a similar background to themselves, might join them in heading out west, and initially they had seemed keen. However it was not to be. Kate could recall the evening when the McElligots broke the news to them. They were all attending a lecture in the parish hall on the then, relatively new invention of Alexander Graham Bell's telephone, and were agog to hear about it. It was during the tea break that a tearful Joan explained that she could not face uprooting again; she felt that it was beyond her strength.

Well, it was a great blow to Kate and John Jo. Their companionship would have been a support in the lonely venture that lay ahead. They called into the church on the way home and prayed for the strength and grace they were going to need. John Jo was anxious then, fearing that Kate's resolution might falter, but she was able to reassure him and this period of their life, so full of hardship and uncertainty, was also blessed with a deepening bond of trust between them.

The day came: all was packed, and left in readiness to be forwarded once they had settled. Kate was particularly glad to see Brigid happily established in a good home, but she, poor girl, had been heartbroken saying goodbye to Vincent who had wheedled a very special place in her heart.

She recalled the faint breeze wafting the familiar malty smell of the grain from the mills and the low whistling of a departing steamer on the lake, as they closed the door on their Buffalo home for the last time. It was with a growing belief and trust that they were in God's hands accompanied by much excitement on the part of the boys, and a sense of calm optimism from John Jo, that they set their faces toward those still untamed regions of the west where they were to forge a very different kind of life for themselves.

CHAPTER [6]

Casper Wyoming 1886-1887

"In the sweat of thy face shalt thou eat bread, till thou return unto the ground; for out of it wast thou taken: for dust thou art and unto dust thou shalt return."

Genesis Ch. 3 Vs. 19

Manual work is central to the life of a Cistercian and for many of the sisters this is a great penance, particularly the physically gruelling work of potato picking. However, though her back had ached from the bending it had not been such hard work for Kate as that, to which she had grown accustomed during those early days in Wyoming.

"HOW SHALL I tell you of those years, of that elemental land full of splendour where God's presence was so immediate?" Kate had said in response to Vincent's eager hunger for information.

It was early spring when they arrived in Cheyenne. This was to be their last link with civilisation, not that this was much in evidence at the time. Every second building appeared to be a saloon, and though they lodged in a respectable house, the sounds of drunken revelry and profanity went on well into the early hours of the morning.

"Ten years ago Kate, stabbings and murders were daily, sometimes hourly occurrences here," John Jo told her, "and it was only the rough justice of vigilance groups that hacked out a modicum of respectability within the town. At one time they disposed of one hundred and twenty of these ruffians within a fortnight. Its considerably more respectable now," and he pointed out the lavish homes of the cattle barons and their fine club, along with other signs of the substantial future that lay before the town. Nevertheless Kate was glad to leave behind the noise and the dirt, and what to her were chilling sounds of debauchery and drunkenness.

She and Vincent travelled to Casper by mail coach on the old Oregon trail three days after John Jo and the older boys, with Billy Joe (their newly hired ranch hand) set out with a freight team carrying most of their household necessities, together with the three cows which were to provide them with milk, butter and cream during the coming months. John Jo had been to Cheyenne to file their claim and stake out the land a number of times over the previous autumn and winter. He had supervised the building of what was to be their solid timber home, and it was now sufficiently complete for them to move into. Kate noted the bleached bones of oxen and other animals along the trail as they passed, and the solitary little mounds with crude headboards marking the graves of the thousands who had died on that very trail. They had been making their way to Oregon and California, and many of those who died were children. She prayed for their souls thinking of her own little Kath and Edie, and cried for those who had loved them, but were forced to abandon their little graves with only the wild winds to croon a lament over them.

"We will never know the full story," she told Vincent, "of the untold hardships faced by those first settlers. Sometimes with little or no preparation, they set out in slow moving wagons, and indeed in some cases with only handcarts, on a journey of two thousand miles over rough tracks. They endured the scorching sun and stifling dust filled heat of summer, and the freezing temperatures and biting blizzards of winter. They were beset by wild animals, hostile Indians, disease and malnutrition. What pain and sorrow they must have suffered. In the torrential rain of spring and early summer tracks became muddy rivers and wagons sometimes became mired for days, and of course, many of their animals were swept away in the flooded creeks and rivers. Indeed many people also lost their lives this way."

She remembered telling him about this as a little boy on that first journey, and recalled how he had interrupted her. "Look Mam at the funny little dog" and he pointed, entranced, at his first sight of a prairie dog standing sentinel on the rim of the circular little fort that was its home. Then they both collapsed laughing as Tim Bailey the driver pulled up the coach and gave chase to a sage hen which seemed to keep one step ahead of him, and then stopped, astounded, when poor Tim tripped and fell flat on his face. However quick-witted Tim stretched and caught him and returned triumphantly with a good supper!

John Jo met them with the buckboard at Casper bridge, near the old fort – it was to be two more years before John Merrit and his hardy band of settlers would lay the foundations of what was to become their local town of Casper. As yet there was no settlement there. They travelled the last seven or eight miles over a rough rutted track to their new home in East Elkhorn Creek at the foot of Mt Casper. The gullies notching the steep rectangular escarpment were cast into relief by the evening light and Kate found comfort in their promise of beauty and shelter. She had been visited by a growing sense of desolation on the lonely track which barely kept at bay the surrounding wasteland of scrub, where only cactus, sagebrush and greasewood flourished and the intimidating vastness of the prairies stretched away to the horizon. The bleakness and isolation of the landscape weighed heavily upon Kate and she fought a temptation to panic. John Jo with characteristic optimism envisioned all transformed into rich agricultural land, and Vincent was full of delight at being allowed to hold the reins for a bit. As they approached the foothills of Mount Casper and the little valley of Elkhorn Creek came into view, she could see their new home sheltered from the loneliness of the plains by a little hill to their rear and she felt a sense of relief and even joy. Bare, but solid looking, it perched on a level area of high ground some hundred yards above the creek. It faced south and was, to some extent, sheltered behind by low hills. There was a comforting stretch of oaks, aspens and cotton-woods along the creek, and when it was still, the sound of water over the pebbles was gentle and soothing.

Her panic subsided and she warmed almost immediately to their new home. It was a long, low building with the kitchen and living room to the right of a central hall, behind which lay a pantry and storm shed. This had a back door that gave on to a grassy incline, and to the left of the hall was a door into the little parlour, with a good sized window facing south and full of light. Behind this was a corridor running the full length of the house which gave access to two good sized, and one small bedroom. "You boys shared one room while your father and I had the other one", she told Vincent. Hattie Dooley, whom John Jo had hired to help her get settled and put the house in order, had the small bedroom. Hattie was to remain with Kate for the first three years, after which she married a stockman from one of the big ranches, but would return to help her out at various times right up to when Kate finally left Wyoming.

"Well Kate, what do you think?" John Jo had been justly proud of his creation, the construction of which he had su-pervised while sleeping rough in the claim shanty (erected to mark the initial claiming of the land). This was down from the house, nearer the creek, and was to become known as Billy Joe's bunkhouse, and indeed he had made it very snug and weather tight. Billy Joe McNabb was their first hired hand, who stayed with them during all her years there, and continued on with Jack until poor health meant he had to move to Denver.

She looked around that first evening at the bare boxes piled high. She could see the dust sparkling under the rays of an evening sun, and was struck by the complex array of emotions illuminating all the faces. Pat looked lost and uncertain, and even Jack seemed confused and bewildered now that they had finally arrived. Louis was characteristically restless, and John Jo was gamely hanging on to the courage and optimism that had fuelled the whole enterprise. Kate recalled looking around those beloved faces, and feeling daunted by the huge unknown that lay ahead. She prayed that she would not fail them, and remembered drawing breath, before she said, "Well this is fun, we are now proper pioneers, let's get the campfires burning." John Jo had grinned and sighed with relief as he sent them all scurrying for wood and water, and confidence and zest was restored. She laid an old sheet on the dusty table and they set out the food they had brought with them. They had a merry feast on the bread and butter, ham, cheese and the rich round fruit cake their Buffalo friends had pressed on them at parting, for they were all very hungry. The boys explored a little before lying down on their bed rolls, while John Jo saw to the horses and cattle. Before they slept that night, they stood together watching the sun setting behind Mt Casper, whose impassive face, softened by the indentation of mysterious gullies was illuminated by the setting sun. As darkness fell and the silence deepened stars began to emerge. Gradually they became encased in a dark mantle studded with minute gems of light and colour. John Jo put an arm around Kate's shoulder, and they both felt a little cowed by the immensity and loneliness that surrounded them.

Kate smiled at Vincent's eagerness to hear all about their adventures, and about the lawlessness and fearful fights and murders that characterised Wyoming then. However, she told him, that while that was all there, the overriding experience of those years was that of the grandeur and terrifying power of nature, of her solitary life within it, and of the hard relentless work of the ranch. It was through this experience that her own soul was honed for the rigours of the contemplative life to which she was to be called. She thanked God for it.

The tyranny and the terror of the weather took them all unawares, in spite of the warnings of Billy Joe and Hattie. They had never imagined such ferocity - such cruel indifferent power. She remembered the still, sunny afternoon in the late spring a couple of years after their arrival; Kate was transferring seedlings into a bigger tray, readying them for planting out and watching Billy Joe cutting logs to replenish their stock. Stripped to his trousers and braces, and with mighty swings of the axe, he split the logs down the middle using an iron wedge as needed, but hardly breaking the hypnotic rhythm of swing and chop. She could recall the muscles of his back rippling and gleaming with sweat, and the sun illuminating the pale insides of the logs as they divided.

He straightened suddenly, looking keenly to the north western horizon where there was a slim bank of dark cloud, and he came quickly to the door asking, "Where is Mr Corbett and the boys Ma'am?" He looked anxious. She told him that John Joe was fixing the fence in the lower field and that Pat was helping him while she thought that Jack was hunting rabbits further up the creek. "Why Billy Joe, what's the matter?" she had asked. "There's a storm coming Ma'am, and it's best get everyone home quick. It will be a bad one," he replied. Kate had looked disbelieving, but he paid little heed. "I'll tell the master and Pat to get back to the house and I'll go for Jack." He quickly saddled his mustang and Jack's bay, flung on his jacket and, snatching a couple of sacks, set off up the hill, stopping to warn John Joe and Pat on the way. Having milked the heifers, they had barely fed and stabled them and the horses when the sky darkened swiftly and the wind rose dramatically whipping the first light snowflakes away. Within minutes the snowfall had accelerated until every sight and sound was obliterated. It became intensely cold, and the snow became like hard ice dust that filled the eyes and ears, so that folk and animals caught in it were deafened and blinded.

Kate was in shock, her Jack was trapped out in that trackless waste. It had only been by dint of constant shouting and calling that John Jo and Pat had been able to find their way to the back door. When she told them about Jack, she had to hold John Jo back from what would have been a futile and dangerous attempt to find him. She fell to her knees before the picture of the Blessed Mother, and prayed over and over with the intensity of desperation, that prayer first voiced by St Bernard in which she had such faith: "Remember, O Blessed Virgin Mary, that never was it known that anyone who fled to thy protection was left unaided...."

John Jo kept watch in the storm shed. The temperature had fallen to below thirty degrees; it was two agonised hours later before Billy Joe banged on the door and carried Jack into the warm kitchen, wrapped in his own coat. They were both suffering from the beginnings of hypothermia. Kate folded them quickly in warm blankets, put heated stones wrapped in old jerseys at their feet, and made them drink warm sweet coffee. Thankfully, they came to no harm. Pat, she remembered, had, with great presence of mind, tied the clothes line around his waist, and had Hattie hold the other end while he took the horses to the stables. He fed and wiped them down, before locking the stables and making his way back to the kitchen by means of the rope and Hattie's tugs. After this experience they linked up all the outbuildings with the house by rope, and indeed this was their method of getting around the ranch on the many, many days when their world was obliterated, and they were marooned in an impenetrable hostile universe.

The winters of 1886 and 1887 were among the most severe recorded in Wyoming. Many human lives were lost and thousands of cattle died on the range, unable to feed through the months of freezing snow. Indeed, nearly every year between the end of March and the end of April, they had severe snowstorms and sometimes Casper would run out of supplies and all business would be suspended. Trains and transport of all kinds would come to a standstill. She could recall a particularly bad one in February 1891, when she tried to dissuade John Jo from joining the other homesteaders, going out to assist the herders on the open range.

"John Joe," she had said, "you are over fifty years of age, and nobody will expect it of you. There are many young men who can help," but he was determined to go. "If our boys were out in this freezing snow and wind," he said, "I would want everyone who could, to go to their aid, I can do no less for others."

Kate had listened with dread to the splitting and breaking of the snow laden branches around them, and the screeching and howling of the wind as she awaited his return. Even in the kitchen with the fire going, the bucket of water by the door was frozen and had to be brought close to the fire to melt. Later on as the wind quietened, she could hear the yelping of coyotes not far away, and the mournful howling of the wolf. It was near eight o'clock when he got back, utterly exhausted and frozen.

They profited by the harsh lessons this taught them, in that they determined to provide winter quarters for their stock, and ensured that they had supplies of feed to see them through these tough months. Up until then cattlemen tended to rely on the open range for feeding during the winter. They were also fortunate in that those first years were spent building, fencing, clearing and planting the ranch, and they did not begin to stock it until the summer of 1889. John Jo and the boys spent much of their time working for the big cattle ranchers in Laramie country, learning the business and earning money, which not only paid for their everyday needs, but also allowed them to put some by for the purchase of feed and stock later on. They were further cushioned by the income earned by John Jo as a land agent. He set up office in Casper in June 1889 dealing in the sale of lots of land in the coal and oil belts then opening up all around Casper. This ensured that he was well placed to locate and purchase the additional land needed to make his own ranch secure and viable. Consequently they did not suffer the huge losses that were the lot, not only of the big cattle men, but sadly, also of their fellow homesteaders.

The misery of the homesteader's lot was exacerbated by summers of searing heat, scorching winds and severe drought. This heat was stifling and they longed for the lazy moaning wind that preceded the frenzied storms and sheeting rain, which, while they left damage in their wake, also brought the blessed relief of fresh air. Too many men and women went bankrupt and had to sell up and abandon their homesteads at that time. Kate recalled the pain of that last visit to Hattie's parents, Jim and Elizabeth Dooley, who were among those unable to carry on. The neighbours had gathered to buy what they needed at the sale of farm equipment, and she retained an image of the weary slumped shoulders, the calloused hands and broken fingernails which bore testament to their years of back-breaking labour in the stubborn fields. Their little four roomed log cabin had always been spotless, and made attractive with cheerful multicoloured rag rugs on the floor, and family photos nicely framed with pine cones on the walls and always a clean fresh tablecloth on the table. Sadly, by the time they made that last visit, both they and the little house looked defeated, their courage had finally crumbled under the dual scourge of the drought filled summers and blizzard torn winters.

However, when not anxious about the family, Kate could marvel at the grandeur of a world stilled, and completely silent under its heavy shroud of snow. Then they would find tracks of deer, wolves and even bears, very close to the house where every footprint and wheel-mark had been obliterated, and even the sound of the creek was bound over to silence by chains of ice. She grew to relish this solitude, broken only by the lonely call of the coyote, with a zest that was muted by the knowledge that it brought suffering to so many.

Kate wanted Vincent to know something of the splendour that surrounded them, as it was this, in combination with the solitude, which forged in her an abiding sense of the 'divine' in the world, and a relish for its contemplation. It was here, that her feet were firmly planted on the contemplative path, and she came to know that nothing else would ever satisfy that thirst.

She had initially panicked a little, faced with what felt to her a rather frightening isolation, and it was some time before she came to fully embrace the solitude and hardships of their new life. The steep fir-clad slopes of Mt Casper to the south were washed by an ever changing palette of colour throughout the seasons. The words alone – crimsons, purples, vermilions, indigos, violets, and such delicate silvers – could not, she said, convey the glory. Serrated all along its' north face by gullies and fissures it gleamed under a tide of colour, and was as suddenly quenched to an ashy paleness when the sun disappeared. So many images came vividly to her mind – the way in which the gorgeous hues of the Rockies intensified as the sun rose, throwing the blue gloom of the stately pines into relief. From a little way up the mountain they could see the bleak wasteland of the prairie transformed into rolling waves of misty gold in the autumn sunlight; those still frosty moonlit nights when the panorama of the starry heavens touched them intimately. "Lord, what is man that thou art mindful of him, or the son of man that thou visiteth him?"

John Jo, with the help of the boys and Billy Joe, worked very hard all through that first spring and summer to make the ranch shipshape. There were stables to be built, land to be cleared of scrub and rocks and then fenced, irrigation channels to be planned, and some land made ready for planting crops and vegetables, as well as the horses and cows to be seen to. Alongside this, John Jo, Jack and Pat worked with the big ranches, particularly during their busy calving and branding seasons. They helped out neighbouring homesteaders, knowing that this would be reciprocated, when they needed help in turn. By autumn, the stables and outhouses were finished, the fencing had begun and all were glowing with health. John Jo's sense of pride and hope was palpable and Kate was gladdened.

She told Vincent a little about Billy Joe and Hattie, who were to prove invaluable supports in building their new lives.

Billy Joe had learnt his trade as a cowboy on the "long drive," when the Texan cattle barons drove their huge herds up from Texas to the rich pastures of Montana and Wyoming, where they could avail themselves of the liberal free range laws and had easy access to the Chicago markets. Like all successful cowboys then, he could turn his hand to anything and indeed they had reason to be grateful for his skill over the years. He kept the ranch and wagons in good repair, and many was the sick or injured horse and cow healed by his skill. He was ever on the alert for rattlesnakes, and taught the family how to detect their hiss and strike before they had time to coil. He must have killed hundreds around the ranch during those early years, and she thanked God that none of them had ever been bitten. Billy Joe seemed to take a liking to the family, and John Jo could not have done without him at that time. He was shy of women, but his initial unease with Kate gradually left him and, when finally persuaded to abandon his bachelor cookstove in the old claim shanty and eat with them she knew he felt he belonged. Both he and Hattie came to be more friends than hired hands and indeed, during those first years, they were their teachers.

Hattie Dooley was the second eldest daughter of a homesteading neighbour who struggled to prove up on his claim with no sons to help and few financial resources. Mr Dooley, a truly good and decent man, had been glad of the little money Hattie could earn, but as a strict Presbyterian he was concerned about her spiritual welfare in what, Kate knew, he initially regarded a little fearfully, as a "Papist home." She told him that it was their practice to say the rosary together nightly and to say their morning and evening prayers privately, and asked how he would want them to support Hattie's religious practice. This direct approach seemed to relieve his mind and they arranged that Hattie would go to her room to read scripture during the rosary. She remained with them from Monday through to Saturday afternoon and returned on Sunday evening. A shy, plain girl, she taught Kate almost everything she needed to know about her new role as a homesteading wife and mother, and Kate became very fond of her.

Indeed, she had a lot to learn. Alongside the endless sewing and knitting involved in making and repairing clothes for four men, and the familiar cooking, cleaning and polishing, she learnt to milk, to separate out the cream and make butter and cottage cheese, to plant out and grow potatoes and vegetables, and to raise poultry – chickens, ducks and turkeys. By the end of that first year in Wyoming, she could make sausages and render lard from their own butchered hogs, as well as preserve eggs and make her own chutneys, pickles and preserves. Come the end of autumn, Kate was always gladdened by the sight of her pantry shelves bulging with a rich array of jars, their little galvanised lids lined with porcelain, and the rubber rings sealing in the goodness of the fruit and vegetables.

Those first years of mind numbing weariness and aching limbs left her with little energy to attend to the hollow wells of misery left by the loss of her little girls and she was glad of the toil. She came, she said, to find joy in her usefulness and to see "the Lord's hand" preparing her for the life He had in store for her.

Each of the boys, she told Vincent, responded differently to those early months in Wyoming. Her earliest memory was perhaps about two months after they arrived. She had tried to establish a routine in order to give some rhythm to their days, and Monday was wash day. It was a clear sunny morning, the air pungent with the aroma of sagebrush following a night of heavy dew, and Hattie had helped her to bring the big tub outside. She kilted up her skirts and worked up a substantial lather which Vincent had great fun with, blowing the bubbles toward poor Shep who was not pleased. Kate shooed him away, and later, laying out the shirts and bedclothes to dry on the warm ground she noticed him a little way from her lying face down, so still, almost hidden in the long grass, watching prairie chickens pecking around their anxious mother while a striped garter snake rippled by him between the grasses, its tongue flickering. She recalled the clutch of fear, though she learned subsequently that these were in fact harmless, and he had been surprised when she hugged him to her.

He had delighted in his new world, and spent hours with Shep, his mongrel sheep dog, fruitlessly chasing the big jack rabbits with their quivering noses and round amazed eyes, and the little chubby gophers that were everywhere. He had a small grey pony, Jenny, which Jack taught him to ride, and how excited he had been that winter when Billy Joe hitched the little sleigh he had made to Jenny, and he had his first sleigh ride.

Jack, too, had taken to the new life with ease and exhilaration, and quickly mastered the range of skills needed for life in the west at that time. He became a skilled horseman and within a short time could navigate his way through the surrounding prairies and the badlands that adjoined them. In fact so skilled was he that in the summer of 1888, though not yet seventeen, he was employed as guide by a Nebraska firm of oil promoters working in the Rattlesnake and Poison Spider fields west of Casper. Kate recalled his excitement when he returned home following the completion of their annual assessment of the Wyoming oil fields. "I found an 'Indian mummy' when we were camping at Emigrant Gap" he told them. "It was lying on the rocks; he had been blown down from a tree with his legs folded back at the knees and his moccasins looked new. His face and body was all dried up and shrunken but his hair was shiny and black and he had coils of copper wire round his arms." Kate and John Jo were surprised, because while they had heard that some Indian tribes laid their dead on trees or platforms to protect them from scavenging wild animals, they knew it was not so in that area because of its nearness to the Oregon trail. The conflict between Indians and settlers along this trail meant that it was more common for them to bury their dead in the ground where they would ride their horses over and back to obliterate all trace of the freshly made grave. "What did you do with him?" Kate had asked. "I sold him to some of the other men for a dollar and they're going to exhibit him in Nebraska,"

Jack replied. This had upset Kate and she had been sharp with Jack, reminding him of the respect due to all human creatures made in "the likeness of God."

Ranching, however, was to be Jack's great love. He had earned the respect of the other cowboys and stockmen as an unusually skilled and competent horseman, and was well liked by them for his quiet unassuming ways. She recalled his excitement, not many months after their arrival, when the tall quiet lad raced home ahead of John Jo from his first big cattle round. "Oh Mam, it was grand. We had to ride right up into the mountains to flush the cattle out of the canyons and gullies, and we had to leap over fallen trees and cross loads of rivers. Sometimes the path was barely as wide as the horse, and high over deep ravines, and once when Firebird [his lovely bay horse] would not cross, I had to get off and lead her across swimming. There were about a thousand cattle all told to be rounded up."

"There were, Kate," John Jo had followed him in, "and these were pretty wild beasts, most of them more at home with the wild bear and mountain lion than with humans. At times we went near nine or ten thousand feet up, it was beautiful, crisp and frosty. Coming down was difficult at times, especially in the wooded areas where you had to steer between living and dead trees to avoid bringing a heavy bough down on your head, or the horse snagging on the fallen branches. Mind you, it was a grand sight when we eventually got down towards the plains. The huge bulls, shaped almost like buffaloes, bellowed and roared, but it was the cows with the yearling calves you had to watch."

"At one time, Mam," Jack took up the tale, "just when we thought we had them pretty well corralled, two of the leaders took fright and set us a terrible gallop, so that we had to try and head them off at the mouth of the canyon." "Bedad, Kate," John Jo said, "I don't deny that I quailed a bit when we stood sentinel there and watched those waves of powerful beasts surging towards us. It took all our strength to steady the horses. But thanks be to God, between our own bellowing, the dogs barking and the thunder of the horses hooves, we were able to turn them back," and Jack smiled proudly as he added, "Your son fairly earned his spurs today."

He revelled in the excitement of it all, and admired the skill of some of the experienced cattlemen and horses who did the close corralling work with these often dangerous animals. "I saw one cow toss a poor dog in the air twice when she felt her calf to be threatened, Mam, and another lunge repeatedly at one of the cowmen, getting her horns right under the horse's stomach but the horse just reared and spun aside at the last minute." "Their skill and coolness is astounding, Kate," John Jo added. "They wheel and turn and seem to gauge by instinct just when to turn aside and stay free of those lethal long horns."

But while Jack was revelling in his new life and freedom and was indeed fast becoming John Jo's right hand man, it was not so for Louis and Pat. Pat was a quiet and imaginative lad, at home with books and music and there was little time for either, in the homesteading life of that time. Kate knew that he was bitter at being removed from a way of life upon which he had thriven in Buffalo, and transplanted to what, for him, was a cultural wasteland. John Jo, aware that he did not relish the physical challenges of ranching, had suggested that he undertake a training in smithy work, this being a service for which there was a considerable demand, and he had rather listlessly agreed. She had watched in dismay as he increasingly withdrew into himself, and his character became resentful and sullen.

In the middle of that first summer she had wandered down to a little dell, where the creek curved around a soft green sward where she hoped to make a flower garden one day. It was a lovely day, and some white butterflies hovered around her as she followed the shimmering flight of two dragonflies on the creek. It was then that she saw the corpse. It was a jack rabbit, with swarms of flies gorging around a bullet hole. Bemused, she glanced up the hillside, and was astounded to see it strewn with the corpses of jack rabbits and gophers. They only shot what they needed for food, and this uncharacteristic and mindless cruelty unnerved Kate because she knew it was Pat even before she confronted him. She could recall his expression of misery and shame: "What else is there to do?" he had muttered, and they knew then that they would have to make different provision for him.

John Jo corresponded with their old friend Cornelius Murphy in New York about opportunities for someone of Pat's abilities. Cornelius wrote to assure them that he could help him get a start with his bank if he passed the required exams. Meanwhile, Kate had established that it would be possible for Pat to get the tuition he needed at the Academy of the Holy Child Jesus in Cheyenne on a weekly basis. This school had been founded by the church in 1885, and was by then well established. So, it was arranged that he would take the weekly freight train on Mondays, and lodge there before returning to the ranch on Friday night.

She remembered the evening they told Pat. They had finished their meal and he had gone into the parlour where he was picking out a tune from the old Bunting collection. She could see his expression reflected in the little mirrors inset into the old piano, softened by his absorption in the tune as the evening light danced over the black and ivory keys. They closed the door behind them and told him of the plan. Pat went very quiet and rather white. After a while he said, "I've been hating it here, everything about it – the loneliness, the monotony, nothing to do," and he added very quietly, "I have been hating you mostly, blaming you." Then he broke down and it was pitiable to see his misery. When he had quietened, she spoke a little about our need for God's help in managing these powerful feelings to which we can all fall prey, so that they do not destroy ourselves or others.

Pat eventually went to work in New York, and some years later was to carve out a name for himself as a singer and actor when he left the bank to work full time as a performer.

Neither had Louis been happy, but for different reasons. He wanted to be with John Jo and Jack working the cattle on the neighbouring big ranches, but Kate felt that at barely thirteen he was too young. He was a restless, impressionable lad and she wanted to protect him a little longer from what could be a very rough, coarse world. The cowboys and stockmen were not bad men, but there were many who through lack of care and good parenting, were of a bleak and crude cast of mind and she feared their influence on one of Louis' temperament. He was sullen and trying during those early months, and he also missed his friends in Buffalo and his sporting activities.

This was a time when they were turning over in their minds the offer that had come from Clare, and coinciding as it did with Louis' restlessness, the decision they came to was not surprising.

CHAPTER 7

The offer From
Clare ...Decision time

"Wisdom is the principal thing; therefore get wisdom: and with all thy getting get understanding."

Proverbs Ch. 4 Vs.7

At harvest time the Sisters worked alongside two workmen. How Kate relished the task of preparing and taking their lunch down to them knowing the hunger of hard working young men. They would rest under the lovely old oaks and beeches that bordered the glinting stubble of St. Benedict's field, and their healthy welcome for the food would bring to mind the memory of her boys.

KATE HAD SENSED a measure of anxiety in Vincent's tentative query, "Why was I the one chosen to be sent home?" She was glad that he had used the phrase "sent home:" had he said "sent away" she would have worried that he had somehow felt less loved.

He was her baby, and she had never been apart from him until she sent him, aged barely eight, to be brought up by John Jo's brother Tom and his wife Ellen. John Jo used to speak of Tom as "a hard working enterprising farmer," full of the new confidence then abroad in rural Ireland. In the 1860s he built a lovely spacious farmhouse, and she remembered how surprised she had been when they first visited. Ellen eyed her sardonically. "Confess, Kate," she said. "You thought we lived in a whitewashed cabin?" She had laughed "No, but I certainly had not appreciated what an elegant home you have" she replied. It was a four bay, gabled house with dormer windows facing south. The generous lawn was enclosed with rows of chestnut trees, and there was a stand of mixed woodland to the right. She loved the way the graceful avenue curved through this to the gravelled half moon which fronted the house, and how the wisteria insinuated itself around the beautiful Georgian door and fanlight, and along one of the windows. It had a distinction and charm, rare then, within the Irish farming community.

Kate liked Tom and Ellen very much. He was hard working and ambitious, but with a passion for justice that she admired, and a real compassion for those of his neighbours and kinfolk who fell upon hard times. Tom was a rate collector for the Tulla Union and she liked to think that he used his influence to mitigate the lot of the many struggling in the aftermath of the famine years. Ellen also was a woman of kindly and charitable disposition. Kate felt keenly her pain at being unable to have her own children, but appreciated the deep faith with which she tried to make her life fruitful bringing comfort to neighbours and friends. The need for this was everywhere then, as the countryside all around was just emerging from the harshness of the hungry years and the upheaval of the land agitation.

She remembered the delicately worded letter clearly: "We have come to accept our sorrow at not being blessed with a child ... would like to be allowed to raise one of your sons with a view to their inheriting ... know well the sacrifice that this would mean ... a trust that we would surely regard as sacred." There had been reassurances too for John Jo who would have known the background: "You might be worried John Jo, knowing the turmoil and trouble there has been in Clare, what between the famine, the evictions and all the land agitation, but things are much more settled now, and we have security of tenure and fair rent tribunals. But the best of it is, that before long we will have the right to purchase the land outright, and when that time comes and the legislation is in place, I plan to do so. I tell you this so that you and Kate can rest assured that your son's prospects would be very good indeed."

This had not altogether been unexpected as they had often wondered if such an offer would be made. They knew that Ellen also had nephews for whom such provision would surely be very welcome. However, John Jo and Tom were close, and the sense of "family blood" was strong, so they were not surprised. Kate remembered them both struggling for the right words, in their reply. They wanted to convey their appreciation of the generous offer, but needed to be confident that any arrangement made would secure their son's future legally. They did not want whichever son was chosen to be left hanging on in uncertainty as they grew to maturity, because they knew that this could happen. Though confident of Tom and Ellen's characters and good intentions, they felt that they must do everything they could to protect the interests of their child. Kate in particular was well aware that illness, old age or indeed the undue influence of other people could blight the best of dispositions and intentions.

She could not remember the exact wording of their letter to Tom and Ellen, but she did recall that their reply had been reassuring. They said that it was only right that they should be anxious to do the best for their child, and Tom was very clear about his intention of making a will bequeathing to their son his property when he and Ellen passed away. She recalled that he had added: "The life will not be so hard John Jo, as when we were lads. I have a good man working for me all the time and a local man who comes to help Ellen with the garden and keep the trees around the house in trim." He also wrote that he was "inclined to reduce the acreage under tillage and move more into cattle grazing and fattening stock," indicating that the land was good for this and that there was more money in it.

Remembering his next words, "I can tell you John Jo it makes for a much less wearisome life and, bedad, I'm getting soft," and knowing that this had been the kind of farming that Vincent had done, Kate was glad.

They were very aware of what a wonderful opportunity this would be for one of their boys, but which one? Pat was then almost fourteen, it was hard to envision this dreamy lad anywhere near a farmyard; no one who knew him could imagine him as a farmer. Jack at thirteen was so excited about going to live in what he persisted in calling "The Wild West" that they knew it would be unlikely he would settle for life in Quin. Louis' preoccupations were all about sport. Kate did not think of Vincent. How could she? He was her joy and the heart of the whole family.

Kath and Edie's deaths, preceding and following their arrival in New York, had left her numbed and as close to despair as she had ever been. The depth of her loss revealed the extent to which she had relied on the expectation of their companionship, in that harsh and often aggressive male world that they were entering. She felt very empty and bereft during that awful time when both her little girls died so quickly, she had lived in daily terror that Vincent would also fall prey. Somehow she knew that the older boys would remain healthy but he was still so young, and she watched in agonies of apprehension for signs of the awful contagion. She prayed intensely that he would be spared to them; then, as time went on and her anxiety eased, in gratitude to God that He did not take him from them.

Kath had been a tomboy and had gloried in the freedom of the countryside during that last holiday she spent in Clare. She had learnt how to ride, and had to be coaxed off the pony at the end of the day. Kate remembered Ellen writing: "she would have slept in the stable with it if we had let her." In time she took comfort from these images so redolent of the zest Kath got from her short life. She had a particular fondness for Pat, seeming to be drawn to, and protective of, his other-worldliness, so unlike her own nature. He had been very upset by her death, withdrawing further into himself, and it was Vincent who had helped to pester him back to life. Kate continued to miss her little dark haired, spirited girl for many years.

Edie had been three years older than Kath. She was fair in colouring, and meeting her for the first time she may have seemed a little dull, but her great charm lay in a complete lack of self- preoccupation and in her rich imaginative life. She had been endlessly involved in stories and adventures, either telling or enacting them, and had been wonderfully entertaining. The image of her expressive little face, enthralled by the *Adventures of Tom Sawyer*, which Kate read to her during those early days on board ship, hoping to orientate herself as much as Edie into their new world, remained with her. Indeed her vivid imagination, delighting in every new experience and event had been an antidote to their apprehensions, and played no small part in helping them to remain buoyant during those weeks of preparation. She could smile later and keep company with the memory of her lovable little girl, but it was to be many, many months before her image failed to evoke a sense of unbearable loss for Kate. Kath was just gone seven when she died and Edie not yet nine.

It was her little boy who brought her back from near despair. Her listless indifference was no proof against Vincent's insistent endless demands. She had to respond and so he became the balm that soothed her loss, and gradually life and time exerted their healing influence. Kate needed Vincent so much then that it never entered anyone's head to consider his suitability for the farm in Quin, and certainly neither Tom nor Ellen, no doubt sensitive to their pain and loss, ever indicated that this was in their thoughts.

Kate could remember the occasion when they came to the decision that Louis should be offered the opportunity of taking up his uncle's generous offer. It was on the homeward journey from another memorable picnic, a very rare event then.

The work during the previous months had been brutish, clearing stones and heavy boulders from the land prior to fencing it. John Jo had borne the brunt of this, refusing to let her help him although gaining some assistance from their neighbour Jim Roche. It was towards the end of summer when he announced that the following Sunday they would down tools and head for a picnic at Garden Creek Falls. Sunday came and he hitched up the buggy, singing, she could remember, an irreverent parody of one of Moore's melodies much to Vincent's delight, and the good humoured zest of the occasion infected the whole household.

Kate sent Vincent to fetch a couple of the bleached and washed flour bags which had been unstitched to make rough cloths, and in one of these wrapped the rich, dark porter cake she had made the previous week. It was not often they had porter in the house, but Jim and Ada Roche had arrived with some bottles and a box of Ada's delicious shortbread biscuits to celebrate their first successful cattle sale and she had put a half pint aside, unbeknownst to the men. She always insisted that they drank out of glasses so it had been easy to slip a jug into the cupboard when she was pouring. Since coming to Wyoming she had become slightly obsessional about such refinements, possibly afraid of being swamped by the roughness of living all around them. She cut slices of home-made soda bread and buttered them thickly placing cold boiled beef and some of her own apple chutney between them. She filled two billycans with hot sweetish tea which she wrapped in another flour-bag cloth to keep warm, and filled two large bottles with milk – these would keep cool in the creek. The remainder of Jim and Ada's shortbread completed the provisions which indeed were lavish in those frugal early days. She sent Pat to get a couple of old blankets from the chest and a rough sheet, made out of those same serviceable flour-bags stitched together, to serve as a table cloth.

Meanwhile the boys had stowed jam jars with string tied around their rims, under the driver's seat, and John Jo fixed his fishing tackle to the outside of the buggy. They set off in fine fettle with Vincent sitting between John Jo's knees holding the reins. It had been a beautiful day, warm and sunny with a light breeze and not too hot. They set down in a shady area at the foot of the falls, with the dark pines rising out of the rocky terrain to either side of the creek. Having un-harnessed and tethered Bob, John Jo wandered downstream with his rod looking for a place to fish. Vincent took off his shoes to go paddling, and the older boys set off to clamber over the rocks jutting out from either side of the falls.

Kate noticed a luminous little blue butterfly settling on a low bush beside her while a large brown one hovered by the wheel as she laid out the blankets and made a seat for herself against the buggy. She settled down to read Charles Dickens' *Great Expectations* which she had borrowed from Ada Roche. It was a rare spell of shared ease and contentment marking a return of some joy for them. In memory at least, there had been none of the irritation that can often mar these occasions. It was a day of benediction.

After about half an hour Kate saw Vincent crossing the creek gingerly. She caught the fluorescent flash of a tiny little hummingbird as he made his way down the opposite bank to where John Jo was seated smoking his pipe and keeping an eye on the rod. She felt for him as Vincent clambered on to his lap knowing how much he had been relishing the unaccustomed leisure, and she loved him for the kindliness with which he welcomed the little boy and helped him to hold the rod firmly. After about ten minutes Vincent became restless with the lack of response and, fixing the rod in place with boulders, John Jo took him by the hand and came back to the buggy to fetch two of the jars. She heard him talking about making a dam to catch some little fish as they returned together. He scooped the child up in his arms, setting him down at a point where the creek was especially slow.

Kate retained a wonderful image of them both – John Jo with his rolled up trousers and braces hanging down by his side, and Vincent totally saturated as he blithely plonked himself down in the creek. She watched their utter absorption as the sunlight played over their faces and glinted off the water. They were contained for a moment in a translucent bubble of contentment which was rudely burst by the return of the older boys "starving" they said, and they crossed back for what all agreed was a feast. She recalled that the unveiling of the porter cake had evoked a zestful if inharmonious rendition of *For she's a jolly good fellow*.

Kate found it hard to remember why they were so clear that Louis should be the chosen one. Maybe it was because, of the three older boys, Louis himself seemed keenest. He had fond memories of holidays in Clare, of hay-making and rides atop the hayricks back to the barn, and of winning races in the sports events organised by the Temperance society in Ennis. He had become attached to his Aunt Ellen who spoiled him with an endless supply of cakes and homemade lemonade.

Kate was uneasy about these rosy-hued memories, aware of the hard work and grit called for by farming life, with its relentless demands around the seasonal cycle. It was difficult to know whether Louis' fun-loving and competitive character would be equal to the challenge. Of all the boys, he was the one who had seemed to miss Ireland most, though, looking back, she could see that this was largely about his friends and the sporting activities he had enjoyed there. Louis was a talented athlete and there were not as yet, many outlets of a sporting nature available where they lived, and indeed they had little time to search out or support him in this, due to the gruelling demands of work on the ranch.

They wrote to Tom and Ellen about their thinking and they responded enthusiastically. Already fond of Louis, they had been optimistic, anticipating that he would gradually grow into the way of life. The painful decision to let go of Louis was made easier by their generous offer to fund a trip to Wyoming every few years for whichever boy was chosen. This allowed them, Kate told Vincent, to plan for his departure with a sense of adventure and without that awful feeling of finality that might have otherwise been the case.

She did not allow herself to think that she was losing Louis when they gathered on the platform of Cheyenne station to see him off. She recalled glancing down at Crow Creek where the mist was still shrouding the line of trees that flanked it as they walked toward the station, and thinking that the weather at least would not be too different when he arrived in Clare. Louis himself was full of excitement at the adventure of it all, with no sense of the magnitude of the moment. Kate watched him match his stride to that of his father as he left them to board the train, his gangly, stretching body coursing with youthful energy. She did not find herself feeling bereft: She had a very definite premonition that he would be back.

CHAPTER 8

Vincent goes to Clare, 1887

"Father, if thou be willing, remove this cup from me: nevertheless not my will, but thine, be done."

St Luke's Gospel Ch. 22 Vs. 42

Kate liked the silence and solemnity of their meals. They sat along one side of the long tables that extended the length of the refectory, listening to the spiritual reading selected for the day. She recalled the words from Psalm 30 dropping luminously into the pool of light which fell on the tiles in the middle of the room:

"Weeping may endure for a night, but joy cometh in the morning."

KATE'S PREMONITION had been correct. By the summer of 1887 Louis was back in Casper and their little boy was with Tom and Ellen in Quin. She found it painful to think back to that time, though soon the memories came unbidden.

It had been early June when Tom and Ellen set out to collect Louis at Ballycar station. With characteristic thoughtfulness Ellen had written an account of how he was. "Louis arrived lean, and tanned from the journey and looking so handsome Kate. My, how he has grown since he was here two years ago, and full of the excitement of the voyage."

Louis' first letter, though brief, had been redolent of this excitement. "We saw porpoises and a whale, which Father Hennessy said was a humpback, they're huge, Mam." (Fr Hennessy was the brother of an acquaintance in Casper, who befriended him on the voyage) "We played a kind of bowling game on deck when it was fine, and I was the champion. All the men put bets on me and bought me loads of lemonade and sweet biscuits when I won." Kate smiled to remember Louis' love of fun and games, and his excitement when involved in a match of any kind. He was so like John Jo in that respect and also in his love of company.

Ellen was to write to her every fortnight, from the time Louis first arrived to when she left for Dorset to enter the priory. Her love for this good and generous woman grew and deepened over the years, as they shared the care first of Louis, and then of Vincent. It had not always been easy for Ellen, who had so longed for a child of her own, to care so lovingly over the long years, knowing as she did that it was unlikely she would ever have first place in their hearts. Kate would have been happy in her later years to have ceded this to Ellen who had so well earned it, but the ties of blood and nature are very strong.

The letters during his first weeks in Ballagh had been reassuring. Ellen had invited her nephews, Fred and Jo, who were of an age with Louis, to stay for a couple of weeks shortly after he arrived. "They had great fun together," she wrote, "hurling in the back field with the two younger Clune boys, and having racing and jumping competitions on the front lawn. Annie," (their housekeeper) "is transformed; until Louis arrived she had been full of aches and pains; there was too much to do in the house, any baking of cakes or puddings had to be coaxed out of her. But now," she continued, "nothing is too much where he is concerned. There's an endless stream of scones, apple pies, fruit cakes, so that we are all getting fat. It's not uncommon to find Louis still in his mucky boots after the milking, leaning against the old deal table in the kitchen –

something that neither Tom nor I would ever get away with – wolfing down freshly baked scones dripping with melting butter. It s a sight, Kate, to see stocky, square Annie in her voluminous apron and old unlaced boots, beaming at your handsome boy bubbling with youth and health. I honestly never thought she was capable of such heights of devotion. Clearly this was a home sorely in need of a child to bring it to life. Indeed, it is not just Annie, but for Tom and myself too, Louis has brought a new lease of life, and we are truly grateful to you and John Jo for having made this possible."

It must have been in early October that Kate began to get the first inklings of unease from Ellen's letters. Louis' own letters were always brief and factual, his enthusiasm coming through when he wrote of a game of hurling, or of his first time going ferreting with some of the local lads behind Quin Abbey. She remembered his words fairly sizzling with the excitement of a week long visit to the spa town of Lisdoonvarna where he gloried in trips to the beach and the wildness of the waves. Tom took him out to the Aran Islands on a Galway hooker, and while he said little about those gallant outposts of Christian civilization, he had been full of the voyage and how he had helped with the cumbersome sails.

His letters in the autumn were more subdued. Kate felt at the time that this was to be expected, as he was settling into a term of schooling at the "Reading House" in Quin, to prepare him for the secondary school after Christmas. This had been Tom and Ellen's proposal, and it had seemed to them a good one. They thought that it would allow him to become acquainted with the subjects he would be studying and prepare him to cope with these. They had also hoped that he might meet some companions there who would move up to the bigger school with him, but this did not happen.

Ellen wrote of Louis being quieter, and initially felt, as Kate did, that this was to be expected. As time went on she began to sense Ellen's concern. Her letters were peppered with anxious comments: "I wish there were some lads of Louis' age around

Ballagh, he misses Fred and Jo," [her nephews], or again, "It's hard for Louis here sometimes, Kate, he misses his brothers." Later, she wrote, "With the days shortening, he's too much in the house with Annie and myself, for you know how he thrives on company. It will be better when he goes to St. Flannans after Christmas. He's already looking forward to the sports and athletics there and Annie and I are trying to teach him cricket which is their main sport. Tom is so busy between the farms and Land League business that he has little time to spare, which is a pity for Louis' sake."

It was in early December 1886 that the floodgates of Ellen's anxiety could no longer contain it. The poor woman had been so concerned about worrying them that she had tried to keep her growing unease to herself, but now it poured out. "Louis," she had written, "has become very quiet and rather listless and I worry that he is unhappy. I have tried to talk to him about it, but he only says that he is fine and that there is nothing wrong." She had spoken to Tom about it, but he was inclined to think that she made too much of it, and that it would pass over. Ellen was not so sure. "I think he misses you all more than he lets on, even to himself," she wrote, "and perhaps especially his brothers and John Jo. A boy of his age needs other boys and he was always close to his father. Tom as you know is a good and kind man, but he is more serious minded than John Jo and does not have that sense of fun and zest which I know Louis relishes. Annie and I love him dearly and he is fond of us, but it's only natural that he should want to be with boys of his own age and with the men." She had also begun to be concerned about whether his nature was suited to the quiet and rather solitary farming life there.

"God knows Kate," she continued, "I don't want to say or even think this, because I don't want to lose the boy. We have all become so attached to him, though I could wish that he and Tom were closer. Don't mistake me, he is genuinely fond of the boy, but their natures are very different, and Tom is too much preoccupied with the politics of the Land League and the Tulla

Union to spend enough time with him. Men are not good at knowing the importance of these things. Louis does try to take an interest in the politics but as you know he is not inclined that way. One thing they do have in common is a love for the fairs. Louis is always ready to get up at the crack of dawn to accompany Tom, even though they enjoy them for very different reasons. Louis thrives on the company, the music, the fights – all the razzmatazz. Tom would keep him by him, trying to teach him how to judge cattle, sheep and so on. He forgets that he is still only a young boy and needs to have fun."

Ellen had hesitated to write all of this to Kate, because she had so wanted things to work out for all their sakes. "I have prayed and prayed about it and eventually went to see Aunt Geraldine," she wrote. "If you remember, she's now Reverend Mother in the convent in Ennis. She is a wise woman and it was a relief to talk to her. It was her suggestion that I should write to you about my fears. She said that they were the 'fears of a true Mother' and that Kate was such a consoling thing to hear, because I do care more about Louis being happy than about myself, and that is a great grace which I know you will understand. May God guide us to do what is best for him."

Kate had not been surprised but agreed with John Jo that it would be sensible to give it a few more months. This would give Louis time to find his feet in St Flannan's after Christmas, and make friends, who might help him settle. Ellen and Tom concurred and Kate wrote to Louis, explaining that they had discussed his future because of his aunt's concern that he was not happy in Clare, assuring him that they all wanted what was best for him. Louis in his reply had indicated that he was often lonely for them and the life in Wyoming which he missed, but had added, "Uncle Tom and Auntie Ellen are very kind to me and I don't want to hurt their feelings." They agreed then that if he was of the same mind after Easter that they would think about him returning, and he agreed to try his best to settle. "It was like the sun re-emerging from a heavily clouded sky," Ellen wrote following this exchange. "He is restored to the fun-loving, light-hearted lad I almost felt we had lost, Kate. He is as good as gold, does everything he can to please his uncle and to make Annie and me laugh at his antics. He is at such pains to thank us for being kind to him, as if this was any hardship, but I know in my heart that it is the hope of returning to Wyoming that is responsible for the miracle cure, and while this saddens me, the relief of seeing him back to his old self helps."

Louis did go to St Flannan's and settled, making friends and excelling at sports, but he never wavered from his desire to return to Wyoming. His letters were chatty in tone and gave them brief accounts of what he was doing, but he repeatedly asked for news of what was happening in Casper and what Jack and Pat were up to.

While they were writing to and fro, pondering what was best to do, John Jo said to her one evening, "You know, Kate, Vincent would be better suited than Louis to take up life in Clare. He's young enough to settle in and gradually get used to living there." He said no more then, but had looked at her so compassionately, that she knew he had been deliberating on it for a long time. She had cried quietly for more than an hour, and he held her hand and let her. Looking back, she believed that she had known in her heart that this was so, but until then could not bear to let her mind dwell on such a possibility. She had also begun to be anxious about Vincent's education, or rather the lack of it, and more worryingly about the influence of some of the very rough characters around the ranch, with whom he was spending increasing amounts of time. These were not bad men, but they were coarse and sometimes cruel. Just a week prior to this conversation with John Jo, she found him with Black Jack McCarthy and Fred Benson (two of the migrant labourers helping with the clearing of stones from the land), throwing stones at the little slip lizards sunning themselves under the water tanks. The two men had been sharing bets as to who would be the first to kill one of the little creatures. Kate was distressed to see this cruelty and to find her little boy enjoying it. She went out to speak to the men, who were apologetic and sheepish and clearly just very thoughtless.

She also worried about his spiritual formation as there was no Catholic Church or Priest within easy distance. While they made a monthly trip to the Catholic Church in Cheyenne, this was, she felt, very minimal support for his vulnerable little soul. She was rigorous about morning and evening prayers and they said the rosary after tea each evening, but the older boys used to chafe against these disciplines. Though she knew that this was to be expected at their ages, it was not a good example for Vincent.

Kate knew that she could not have opened her heart to the idea of his going if she had not learned to trust Ellen so well over the previous months. She believed that the quality of a child's care in the home was dependent on the mother, and Ellen had shown herself to be capable of such disinterested love over the previous months, able to put Louis' wellbeing before her own wishes and disappointment, that this gave her confidence. She knew Ellen to be a woman of great faith and conviction who would provide Vincent with the emotional and spiritual support he would need. She was also aware that the educational opportunities he would have there were far superior to anything available in Casper at that time. Indeed everything pointed to where their duty lay in providing for his future. So, when she eventually dried her tears, she had been able to answer, "I know, John Jo."

John Jo had been of the opinion that Vincent and Tom were more likely to be suited to each other. "Tom as a boy," he said, "had the same curiosity and interest in everything that our lad has, though Vincent is a lot more engaging." He believed that Tom would become very attached to him, which indeed happened and she remembered him adding, "Then who would not become attached to our lad," and she had noted the pain in his eyes, to which, too preoccupied with her own sense of impending loss, she had given little attention.

Neither John Jo nor Kate had slept the night following this conversation, or indeed had been able to give each other any comfort. They needed to come to terms alone, with the bleak prospect of the loss they were facing.

As with so much else in her life, Kate looked back with gratitude to God, for what she regarded as a major station in her own personal way of the Cross. The contemplation of Vincent's departure felt like a death to her. She did not know then, she told him, that through this breach would flood God's grace, and ultimately his peace and joy. Back then, all she felt was a chilling bleakness and great weariness with a life that seemed to offer an endless procession of sorrows. She prayed for the grace to bear the pain, and for the courage to let him go, if not with gladness at least with the feeling of support for the venture, and without any perceptible hint of their pain which could have been a burden to him. It was a time, Kate told Vincent, when she and John Jo had been given the consolation of drawing closer than they had ever been, in the course of their sometimes troubled marriage.

They spent the next three months or so preparing him for life in Clare and for the journey. They had asked Ellen and Tom to arrange to have a photograph of themselves taken, and sent over. Ellen had, with her intuitive wisdom, included Louis and their fat tabby cat in the picture, which of course made it so much easier for Vincent to warm to. Kate recalled how they had put this up on the sideboard so that he would become familiar with their image, and each evening they would spend time talking about the farm and life in Quin. They had asked Louis to write to him about what he was doing, so that he could gradually build up a picture of what life was like there.

Louis, poor lad, had been worried at first that Vincent was being "sacrificed" in his stead, and clearly felt guilty about the plan. However, over a few letters they were able to reassure him that it was about providing Vincent with opportunities that he would not have in Casper. He was able to appreciate that their main concern would always be for the happiness of their boys, and that, just as in his case, they had paid attention to his wishes so they would with Vincent. He played his part well then, making his letters vivid and interesting for a small boy. He wrote about the old sheepdog, Shep, being tormented by Biddy the fat tabby, and about the excitement of going out, his face blackened, with the wren boys on St Steven's day and being stuffed with lemonade and cakes in all the houses. She had smiled at the memory of his truly mouth-watering descriptions of Annie's baking. On the evenings after they had received one of Louis' letters, Vincent and Kate would sit down at the kitchen table and draw pictures of the stories in them, so that all the time his familiarity with the life at Ballagh was growing.

Kate told Vincent that it had been very hard for his aunt Ellen to be enthusiastic about their proposal when they first broached it. In retrospect, she realised how very apprehensive Ellen must have felt about building up her hopes, and fearful that they would be dashed yet again. The poor woman had suffered so much disappointment over the prospect of losing Louis, that she found it hard to face the possibility of this happening again. Tom too, and even Annie had been bereft. All had invested so much expectation in things working out happily, that it had not crossed their minds that it might not. It was therefore, a very great shock, and besides, they had grown very attached to Louis.

Their generosity in protecting him from any censure strengthened the bonds of confidence between the two households. Tom wrote to John Jo urging that, "no blame be attached to Louis: He's a good lad, John Jo, and I could not fault him. He has tried hard to do everything we asked. I suppose it's hard for a lad of his age to settle for such a quiet backwater when he's had a taste of the excitements of the 'Wild West'. His heart has remained there in spite of our efforts. We will miss him, and I know Ellen will be sore lonely until she gets used to the quiet house again."

Well, they wrote to and fro for a couple of months, sharing their thoughts without reserve. In the end they came to an agreement that, Vincent would go to live with them in order to "acquire a good education", and that they would see how he settled before making any more definite plans for the future. This had been sensible and protected everyone – a little. It made it easier for the eight-year old boy to understand why they needed to send him to Clare, as he had often heard them discussing where they might find a good school for him. It helped Tom and Ellen to take things one step at a time and not to invest too great a weight of expectation in him. For Kate and John Jo, it had helped a little to reduce that awful sense of finality when they came to say goodbye. Plans were made for him to return to Wyoming for a visit the summer before he moved up to the secondary school, which they hoped, would help him retain a sense of connectedness to them.

It had been hard on Jack and Pat, who were quiet when told of the proposal. They worried that he would be lonely, and were only partly reassured by the plan to leave Louis in Ballagh for a month after his arrival to help him settle. For Jack, particularly, it was very tough. There was a real bond between him and his little brother. It was for Jack, an immeasurably seven years older and wiser, that Vincent reserved his total devotion and Jack in turn could always be coaxed from his gruffness by his passionate partisanship. Kate smiled to remember the number of times when John Jo and Jack, locked in mulish conflict, often over Jack's bid for freedom from the endless toil, would find the tension defused by Vincent entering the fray in support of Jack. She recalled the Saturday when he had planned to meet the Bennett boys for a game of handball and John Jo was adamant that he required his help to clear the lower meadow. Jack had been angry and resentful and Kate was too weary to mediate. It was the grace of Vincent's childish words, "I'll help you Daddy, please let Jack go ..." that restored warmth and goodwill, and allowed them to work out a compromise. His departure deepened in Jack an aura of loneliness that he never really shook off.

Kate told Vincent of the board game Pat had devised to help him prepare for the journey ahead of him. He got a square board which he divided up into a large number of little squares, each of which represented a station on the route of his journey between Casper and the harbour at Queenstown county Cork, where Tom and Ellen taking Louis with them would travel to meet him. Using counters and dice, the aim of the game was to reach journey's end as quickly as possible. Pat had found the names of all the stations *en route* and painted them in beautifully. Vincent could faintly remember the picture of Cheyenne station, where Pat had included images of Kate with John Jo and Jack lifting him and his suitcase onto the train. She could not recall the names of many of the stations that she then knew by heart. She did remember the wonderful drawing of the busy Chicago intersection, with long processions of Cattle Wagons drawn up on the sidings, and little "bellow bubbles" coming out of the mouths of the beasts. Here Vincent was required to change trains, and Pat had drawn in, a little boy being shown where to get on the train to New York by the conductor. The picture of Queenstown harbour had Tom and Ellen in it, with Louis jumping excitedly on the quay awaiting Vincent's arrival.

Many was the time Kate blessed Pat and thanked God for that board game as, more than anything, it helped Vincent to become familiar with the daunting journey he had to make and which she had so dreaded. They played it repeatedly during the six weeks before he left, sometimes reversing it, so that the aim was to get to Wyoming from Clare. She believe that this helped him to make sense of the journey and, indeed, it had helped all of them to prepare for his going, and to feel the link between both places, which brought a little ease. She had hoped that it would be a source of comfort to him in his lonely times.

Kate had to pass quickly over that late spring morning in 1887, when she said goodbye to her little boy on the station platform. That image of him, so serious, his new suit a little too big for him, the starkness of the label bearing information about their address and that of his destination, which they hung around his neck would haunt her with acute anguish in the months ahead.

The boys lifted his cases onto the train, while John Jo went to get seats. Vincent was quiet, as if somehow aware that something very big was happening. Kate remembered feeling so cold, though it had not been a cold morning – "cold as the grave," she thought. The boys hugged him, and she hugged him closely for a few minutes before John Jo took his hand and led him into the train ... then he was gone, he waved just once as the train pulled out.

Vincent could sense the anguish this memory evoked for Kate and was aware of her struggle to breathe, before she could continue. She recalled little of the days and weeks after he left. She told him that she prayed constantly for the grace to bear her loneliness for him. John Jo suffered too, as did his brothers, and she believed that it was this sense of shared pain that made them all try for each other, and they were able to get on with their lives.

It was not until they received Ellen's telegram to say that he had arrived safely that they were able to talk about him again. There must have been a shared though unspoken terror that something awful might befall him on the way, and the relief of knowing he was safe had been wonderful

Ellen wrote an account of his arrival: "Vincent was waiting on deck oblivious of the rain streaming down his face while we waved from the quayside. He looked so little Kate, and slightly dazed – and no wonder, after such a long journey and such sights as he'll have seen. I had to hold myself back from rushing to enfold him in my arms when he came down the gangway, as we let Louis go to welcome him. It was lovely to see his serious little face relax as Louis hugged him: what a beautiful boy he is Kate. He then came over with Louis and kissed me gravely on the cheek and shook Tom's hand. You could sense his relief and a growing sense of security as he chatted with Louis about their shared experience on the long train journey back. Tom and I were content to let them talk, and we marvelled at the courage of the little boy."

She had continued: "When we reached Ballagh, Annie had a great fire burning in the sitting room and a lovely tea laid on the table, with ham sandwiches and tiny little fairy cakes with pink icing and a V picked out in white. I must tell you about Annie, Kate. She was, as you know so distressed at the thought of Louis going, that she did not want to hear about Vincent. Louis was wonderful over these past weeks, winning her around with his antics and promise to write to her when he wrote to Vincent, and even to look for a husband for her! This always ended in her chasing him and general laughter. However, she no sooner laid eyes on Vincent than the dormant lioness in her surfaced! I think it was the unexpected "littleness" of him Kate. Louis is now taller than Tom, and Vincent is still such a very little lad. It will certainly be over Annie's dead body that any harm comes to your boy. Indeed he was hardly here a week when all our hearts were won; he is such an endearing child, with a quality of stillness to him that is somehow restful."

Ellen had then gone on to describe how she had "found him in the barn sitting on the ground and looking closely at one of the hens. It was a good five minutes before I drew his attention, asking was he having a little rest?" "No" he said, "I'm waiting for the hen to lay me an egg. Annie says she'll make me a fried egg if the hen lays one." I smiled and explained that they like to be alone to lay their eggs, and he happily took my hand to go in search of another nest, and was ecstatic to find an egg. This easeful quality is something he must have inherited from you, Kate, as it certainly does not characterise your restless John Jo?"

Not long after he had arrived in Clare, their sadness was overlaid by acute feelings of anxiety. News had filtered through from fellow Irish immigrants in Casper that there was trouble yet again on the O'Callaghan estate which was not far from Quin. They knew, of course, of the disturbances there back in the early 1880s, and of the famous battle of Bodyke in 1881. They were worried because Tom had been very involved in the Land League, and might somehow be implicated. They were also aware that Parnell and the Irish Parliamentary party had taken control of the Land League during the previous few years, and that this had served to curb its more violent excesses. In addition, many of the clergy were by then more actively involved in working with the people, and they felt reassured that this would help to keep the country law abiding and peaceful. However this news of a fresh outbreak of trouble just when Vincent arrived in Clare disturbed Kate.

An initial letter from Tom to John Jo did nothing to reduce her anxiety. He had written in stirring tones of how "8000 men gathered daily in Bodyke during the last week of May, in the expectation of evictions commencing," and he continued: "When they finally did start on the second of June, I was at Scarriff fair, when suddenly about mid-morning, there were horns and church bells pealing for miles around. This was the signal that evictions were about to commence. Your blood would have surged, John Jo, to see the way in which every farmer, to a man, left his stock and produce in the care of the women and a handful of boys, and set out for Bodyke. When we got there we must have been at least 5000 strong. The Fusiliers, bailiffs, and of course the RIC were all out in force and, bedad they were fairly edgy when they saw the crowds. Father Murphy and Father Hannon were with us and marched between them and the rest of us, and that checked the wilder boys from having a go at them." He then went on to describe the ferocious resistance offered by the O'Halloran family, which Kate had confessed she would have found inspiring were it not for her frantic worry about Vincent's safety, and of course that of Louis and the whole household.

Well, John Jo must have written to him because his next letter, written to both Kate and John Jo, had been much more subdued and did help to quieten her fears. He explained that the severe economic downturn in 1886/87 had made it difficult for the Bodyke tenants to pay their rents, and that Colonel O'Callaghan was unwilling to compromise and determined to apply the full rigour of the law. He wrote, "You need not be afraid that there will be any violence, Kate, as people now are much more disciplined and confident of ultimate victory. Indeed it was wonderful, the way in which everyone, in spite of the provocation, was so restrained at Bodyke. Of course, Michael Davitt, who came down to lend support, took any pitchforks away from the tenants to avoid, as he said, 'what might be a source of temptation' in the heat of the moment. Also the urgings of the priests had their effect. At one point, when that young hothead Frank O'Halloran was about to forcibly eject a policeman who had got into the house, he heeded Father Hannon's pleadings 'not to do it' and so almost certainly, avoided what would have been an excuse for the Police to open fire."

"I am telling you all these details so that you can be very sure that if people were able to restrain themselves in this situation, where there was such dire provocation, you do not have to worry that violence will erupt. There were twenty-eight tenants, out of a total of fifty-seven, evicted from the O'Callaghan estate, but the joke of it was that no sooner had the bailiffs and police withdrawn than we took down the barricades, fixed the door and restored the walls of the homes affected, while our women folk replaced the furniture and got the fires lighting again: so much for O'Callaghan's victory. Although you know, John Jo, I could find it in myself to feel sorry for the old devil. He's one of those old military types who believe that any attempt by what he calls 'the peasantry' to organise themselves is a crime and should be suppressed. He is tolling his own death knell by his stubborn pride, if he but knew it, and looks so haggard and miserable that it is pitiable."

The one blessing that came out of this period of anxiety for Kate was that the relief of knowing that Vincent was safe made the pain and loneliness she felt for him somehow more bearable. How eagerly they looked forward to his letters which arrived so regularly. Ellen, bless her, had seen to that, and as time went on it got easier, though many was the occasion during that first year when the ache for him would catch her unawares and she cried for his loss to her.

For Vincent too it had not always been easy, and she could readily call to mind the many times when Ellen needed to comfort his confused and lonely little heart. Kate had asked that she let her know about the bad times as well as the good, so that they could share ideas about how best to deal with them. One particularly poignant letter stood out in her memory.

"Tom, Vincent and myself went to the 'point to point' just outside Ennis last Thursday, Kate," Ellen wrote. "We had a wonderful day, Tom and I delighting in Vincent's enthusiasm and excitement. With Tom's help, he shot down a coconut in the shooting gallery and won a coloured ball, and he and his little friend 'Corny' Clune spent ages on the swing boats. The highlight, however, was the pony ride; up and down the field behind the tea tent he trotted happily, and it was only with the lure of tea and cakes that we were able to coax him down. Eventually we set off for home, sleepy and we thought content, when out of the blue he started to cry, quietly at first but then sobbing as if his little heart would break. Tom and I were beside ourselves with worry: we could get no answer to our repeated questions as to what was the matter. We stopped the trap, and I just held him in my lap rocking him back and forth, and feeling, Kate, as if my own heart would break for the child's sadness. It was a good half hour before he quieted, exhausted by the emotion on top of the excitement of the day. Annie had put a hot water jar in his bed, and I carried him up and tucked him in, stroking his head until he dropped off to sleep. The next day he seemed fine, and when I asked him if he knew why he had been so sad, he just said, "Mam did not see me on the pony." I suggested that we should write and tell you about it, and maybe draw a picture of the pony with him on it, and this we did."

Kate had kept that picture for a long time. She sent him back pictures of some of the horses on the ranch and wrote about how he would be able ride them when he came to visit Wyoming in a few years' time.

There were fewer sad times as the first year passed and Vincent settled so happily into life in Clare. There were lovely stories of him and Corny Clune going fishing with Tom in Lough Fin with rods made out of hazel sticks and string; of Annie, bowling for him and Corny on the front lawn, teaching them to play cricket, and a lovely picture of him with his puppy Bran. This had been the puppy he and Louis had chosen a week before Louis was due to return to Wyoming. It had been Ellen's inspired plan, to ease the sadness of Louis's departure for him. They had chosen it the week before he left, and Vincent was to go and pick it up after he had said goodbye to Louis at Ballycar station. Ellen hoped thereby to cushion his sorrow, and indeed it worked, as he was enchanted with Bran and spent the rest of the day playing with him. He even coaxed Annie (by then totally his slave, Ellen wrote) to let him have his bed by the range in the kitchen. His letters for a long time were full of Bran, and Kate had no doubt that he played a big part in comforting her boy during that first year.

For herself, the image of his growing contentment, apparent in the letters from Ballagh, was a bittersweet one. She was glad, of course, and in her deepest heart grateful, but she was, as she said, his mother, and he had been her baby and, "Oh, it was hard." Vincent had ached to comfort her then and had felt a brief surge of anger at the cruelty of the monastic grill that separated them. Sometimes the anguish would surface and seem beyond bearing, she told him, "but by God's grace and the balm of passing time," she grew more resigned and detached from her own grief.

Then the time came for him to return to Wyoming for a visit, and once again Kate was swamped by a maelstrom of emotions. A confused mix of longing and fear had left her drained and almost ill as the time drew near for his arrival.

CHAPTER 9

Vincent's return and John Jo's death 1891-1894

"I have fought a good fight, I have finished my course, I have kept the faith:"

The second epistle of the blessed apostle Paul to Timothy Ch. 4 Vs. 7

More vividly with each passing year, Vincent's face, barely glimpsed through the grill, brought to Kate's mind that of John Jo as a young man, and a surge of tenderness would wash over her.

KATE LOOKED BACK with compassion on the anxiety, bordering on torment, with which she had anticipated Vincent's first visit in the summer of 1891. She had feared that he would harbour feelings of resentment for sending him back to Clare … that she would be accused of a failure of love. She did not talk about this to John Jo but she knew that he sensed her anxiety and was puzzled by it. She remembered praying for peace of mind and the grace to bear any condemnation Vincent might convey.

Then he was there, a shy, strangely familiar, beloved stranger. They met him at Casper station, and he suffered himself to be hugged, slightly awkward, but pleased also, to be so warmly welcomed. Kate's fears dropped away; she was free at last of the ghost of that lonely little child from whom she had parted with such heartbreak, and whose sadness had haunted her over the years since. In his place was a transparently contented and confident boy, soon very much at his ease under the affectionate ribbing of his brothers. She blessed Ellen and Tom for the generosity with which they had nurtured his natural affection for all of them. To see him so confident of his place within their affections was balm to her, and she became aware of a very particular bond developing between him and John Jo.

The rest of the family watched as he and Vincent talked of people and places in Clare known only to both of them, and delighted in shared anecdotes about farm life there. Kate thanked God for this unexpected blessing which allowed her boy to insinuate himself effortlessly back into the heart of the family. She had been so fearful that he would feel an outsider when returning to them. Instead he had not only carved out a very special niche for himself but had rejuvenated John Jo, allowing him to delight again in his own youth. Vincent was of an age to relish the stories and life of the west, and he had a wonderful time on that first visit. He hero-worshipped Jack, whose affection and care of him had been truly heart warming. Jack taught him to ride rodeo and use a lasso with impressive patience, and Vincent's delight in acquiring a measure of confidence was no greater than his. Jack would sometimes take him to the ranch on which he was then working over near Rawlins, and Kate recalled John Jo telling her, "You would laugh, Kate, to see how protective Jack is of him. He went and tore a strip off one of the stockmen, Jock Daly a man in his thirties, for using profane language in front of the lad." He laughed and added, "It was a measure of his respect and liking for Jack, stripling and all that he is, that he took it with good grace and even apologised."

She reminded Vincent of the excitement with which he set out with Jack for a trip to an outlying cow camp. She had watched him pack his saddle bag with supplies of bacon, coffee, salt and pepper, and a freshly baked loaf of bread, with his own little frying pan on top. He had looked so proud, and a lump came to her throat as they cantered away giving a final wave at the gate. He had been fairly sizzling with exhilaration on his return; "It was great Mam" (what a pleasure it was to hear the familiar 'Mam' instead of the formal 'Mother' of his recent letters) "Billy – the cook, roasted a whole side of an antelope over the camp fire, and cooked the potatoes and meat in pots underneath the ground." "Was it good?" Kate asked. "It was the best food I ever ate, and what's more, I lassoed Tenesee Kate when he wasn't looking." She laughed to remember how startled she had looked, and Jack grinned: "He did too Mam, Tenesee Kate is what the cowmen call the new tenderfoot in camp, and you should have seen his surprise when Vincent lassoed him from behind." "No doubt egged on by you," she said drily, and Vincent added happily, "He chased me for ages but could not catch me."

There were times when Jack, Louis and John Jo were away working and Vincent and Kate had time together. She cherished these interludes but after a little he grew restless, and she knew he was missing Clare and his friends. She had been glad of it, for she knew that Tom and Ellen, and indeed she and John Jo also, feared that he might become disenchanted with life there, if Wyoming proved too exciting.

Vincent relished the stories Billy Joe told him of life in the west. He would listen spellbound, to his accounts of battles with Indian tribes over territory, and indeed, if Billy Joe was to be believed, he fought in every one of them! Vincent's favourite was the very gory description of the battle of Little Big Horn in 1876, when the Sioux were victorious, killing General Custer and all his men. He was equally riveted by Billy Joe's hair-raising descriptions of Indian attacks on settlers, complete with lurid details of kidnappings and scalpings. Kate would sometimes catch his eye in the middle of these sagas with a warning look, and he would sheepishly moderate his tone for a while. She remembered Vincent laughing aloud at his account of the Indian women emptying the bags of flour distributed to them by the government into the Missouri, turning the muddy river white. They did not at that time bake or eat bread, only meat, which of course had been plentiful then. They used the bags to make shirts for their men and dresses for themselves. She smiled to remember his disappointment, when on a visit to Casper, a straggling group of Indians driving some old ponies and rickety wagons followed by four or five scrawny dogs passed them. This was greatly at odds with his cherished image of wild Indian warriors of war-like ferocity, but sadly was to become the more familiar one as these once proud people lost their way of life and territories.

It seemed as if Vincent could never get enough of murder, robbery and general ruffianism. He listened avidly to the tales of the Wilcox train robbery, and the gang members' escape to an outlaws' lair just north east of Casper, which the famous Currie gang would later make their base for a time. "Can we get to go and see it, Billy Joe," he had asked, and even that old reprobate looked shocked at such a suggestion. Kate used to worry about his liking for the more gentlemanly robbers such as Otto Chenoweth, and 'Stuttering Dick', always gallant to women, but John Jo only laughed when she mentioned it. "To be honest I kind of like them myself Kate," he had said. She could see that the daring of that rascal Phil Watson, who had been their deputy sheriff in 1889, really took Vincent's fancy. Watson had been one of a very successful gang of horse thieves in the county and had only been caught that year.

Tales of a different kind were those about the paid killers, such as Joe Elliot and Tom Horn, hired out by both stockmen and ranchers during that time. Kate could sense the apprehension with which he listened to these, and would try to hush such talk where she could. It had been a strange time then, when the usual laws and rules of society did not quite fit. This of course had been particularly the case in the wars between the cattle barons and the rustlers. There had been a tradition among the small homesteaders of claiming the odd unbranded calf or wandering steer, and nobody had taken this too seriously. Indeed many of the homesteaders they knew, freely admitted that they had started their modest herds in this way, and it had been generally tolerated.

However, the large ranchers became concerned when the rustlers began to blotch their brands in order to replace them with their own, and to shoot the mothers of calves in order to be able to claim and brand the calves themselves. The year before Vincent made his first visit back to Casper the big cattlemen had offered substantial rewards for any information that would lead to the conviction of the rustlers. They had been unable to secure any convictions because the jurymen, and indeed sometimes the judges, tended to sympathise with the smaller homesteading rustlers. It was then that the ranchers began to take the law into their own hands, and in July 1889, a saloon keeper Jim Averill, and his accomplice "Cattle Kate", known to sympathise with the rustlers, had been lynched in a gully near Jim's saloon, as a warning to would-be rustlers.

Kate recalled Jack telling Vincent the tale of the subsequent battle, known as the Johnson County War, during his visit in 1893. "It happened last March, the cattle chiefs hired twenty-two Texan gunmen and set off for the home of a known rustler. Dad was one of the forty-nine men that rode out with the sheriff to protect the rustlers, everyone was on their side."

She remembered feeling very uneasy as she listened to Jack's partisan championing of the rustlers, and tried to speak to John Jo about it. He had been very dismissive of her scruples. "They are greedy, grasping bullies, Kate," he said of the cattle barons. "They own almost the entire stock of this state, and they grudge a miserable portion of all that wealth to the hard working homesteader trying to make a modest living for his family." "But John Jo," she had remonstrated, "these men have taken the law into their own hands because they could not get any redress through the courts. If the law was upheld we would not have this situation. If everyone just takes the law into their own hands there will be chaos and none of us will have any security." "I know, I know," he had said. "We have to find a better way, and we will, but meanwhile we can't let folk be murdered by hired gangsters." In the event, the military got to the scene in time to prevent a bloodbath, though the rustler's ranch had been burnt down and two men killed.

While tales like these sent a shiver down Vincent's spine, he delighted in discovering that Calamity Jane had been in Casper the previous autumn and had actually been seen by Jack. He had read about her exploits and, Kate remembered, had asked eagerly, "What was she like, Jack?" She had smiled at his crestfallen expression when Jack had replied bluntly, "Horrible – she looked like a man." She recalled John Jo, who was by then a Justice of the Peace, telling her that Calamity had been picked up in a routine round up of the inmates of a house of ill repute where she had lodged in Casper, in the December of that year. The poor soul had a very hard, rough life and by that time had become totally addicted to whiskey, and though she had done some bad things, she had also done many kindnesses and had great courage.

Casper during those years had been a wild and lawless place with many saloons where drinking, gambling, and prostitution were rife and Kate tried very hard to protect her boys from its influence. Jack had an instinctive distaste for this life and had ensured that Vincent was well protected on his visits. She did worry that Louis, who had always been drawn to excitement and novelty, would be more vulnerable. Her prayers for his protection had been answered by his meeting Nellie when still in his early twenties. Nellie, though not Catholic, was a strong minded girl of good character, and came of very decent people. This had proven to be a good relationship and one very protective of Louis' welfare, and she thanked God for it.

Kate cherished the memory of Vincent's happy times with them. They were precious to her, helping to soothe the ongoing ache his departure would again leave behind. She recalled his state of excitement on returning from the mining encampment on Mt Casper, where Billy Joe had taken him to visit with an old friend of his staying there: "You'll never guess Mam, Billy Joe and I went panning for gold. We didn't get any but we're going to try again when Billy Joe has the time," and indeed there had been a find of gold in the spring before he arrived. Mining on Casper Mountain began in 1888 when the lust for gold seemed to permeate the land and folk left good jobs in droves in pursuit of the elusive wealth. In fact there had been gold, silver, copper and galena found on the mountain and, a few years later, asbestos was discovered. Huts and shanties of all kinds sprang up overnight, and for a few years the place fairly hummed with activity.

Kate remembered visiting a young girl who had given birth to a baby boy in one of the rough encampments there, the September after Vincent left. She had looked so helpless and young huddled in some dirty old blankets clutching a surprisingly healthy looking baby to her breast – she could not have been more than sixteen or seventeen - and had been pathetically grateful for the eggs and milk she brought her. They spent the day together getting the place in order, and it had been good to see her courage returning, once she had a good meal inside her. Kate got great pleasure from making little shirts and dresses for that baby for the few weeks they were there, but she never saw the father of the child in all that time. She still remembered to pray for that little family but did not know what had become of them. By the time she left Casper this encampment and all the activity had disappeared, as minerals had never been found in sufficient quantities to make it worthwhile mining. What a lot of disappointment and disillusionment there had been.

The fourth of July celebrations had always been a big attraction. There was a brass band in Casper by the time of Vincent's second visit, in 1893, and he revelled in it all – the bronco busting, the baseball game between Casper and Douglas in which both Jack and Louis had played, though she could not remember who had won. But it had been the races that Vincent had really loved, and indeed horse racing was the most popular sport in Casper in those days. Kate recalled his excitement after the big race: "I won, I won Mam." He came racing over to her waving a dollar bill and hoarse from cheering – "I bet on Doc

Middleton and everyone else thought that Sorrel Jane would win, but me and Jack, we stuck with Doc." This had been a very special race, as two thoroughbred racehorses had been imported for the occasion and normally it was just the horses used by the ranchers and cowboys that raced. Initially there had only been *Doc Middleton* and then, just prior to the race, the reputedly very swift *Sorrel Jane* and a professional Jockey had been brought in to challenge Doc's supremacy. The excitement was intense, with many allegiances veering back and forth between Doc and the newcomer. All the businesses in the town had closed for the day, and everyone was lined up on both sides of the track, straining to keep the horses in sight. The judges stood on large boxes, gazing out over the rough grease-wood and sagebrush flats, where shadows chased themselves under a brisk breeze. Kate recalled thinking that never had the sophisticated courses of her girlhood, Punchestown or Leopardstown, offered greater pleasure than that rough course.

Such days of leisure had been rare then, and not least amongst their pleasures was the opportunity to socialise with their homesteading friends and neighbours. It was these same homesteading neighbours who had provided them with the support they needed to make a go of their new lives. Without it they could not have survived. It was neighbours who showed them the best way of breaking the sod for the cultivation of vegetables and corn, and helped them with seed types, and knowledge about the most effective planting styles. It was they who helped them cut and save their first hay and butcher their first hog, and who advised Kate about what kind of poultry to get and where. They of course, helped them in turn, and became very good friends with some of them. She told Vincent about Jim and Ada Roche, and the Wilmotts, who had been particularly good friends to them.

By the time Vincent made his second visit to Casper he found them successfully established pioneering homesteaders. John Jo had served an eighteen month stint as Justice of the Peace between January 1891 and June 1892 having been nominated on the democratic ticket in the 1890 election, and was a highly respected citizen of his new homeland. They had worked very hard and were proud of their achievements, but realised that they had advantages that many of their homesteading friends did not have. Officially the homestead legislation allowed just one claim of 160 acres per family head, and they knew from the outset that this would not be enough to pasture a herd and grow hay, feed and crops for both stock and family. They had some money and were able to buy up adjacent lots, as well as build the substantial ranch house that allowed them to weather the bitter winter snow storms.

The travel costs had been considerable, but they had been able to bring out enough equipment, livestock and supplies to last them the whole of the first year. Kate remembered thinking that they would never eat all those barrels of cured meat and canned fruit and vegetables, but indeed they did, and a lot more besides. These supplies were topped up by the fruits of John Jo's and the boys' hunting and gifts from neighbours. They were able to hire help, and had enough money to make the improvements they needed, to clear, fence and irrigate the land, and had kept some money aside to buy stock when they were ready. "You may be sorry to hear that we never needed to resort to rustling!" Kate told Vincent with a smile, but added, "We were the lucky ones and it was sad to see the hopes of so many of our fellow settlers reduced to dust, as they were forced to sell up for want of a little capital."

It had been during thanksgiving dinner, later on in that year, that Kate first became aware that John Jo was not well. It had been a particularly merry occasion because Pat was home from New York for a few days, and they were joined by Jim and Ada Roche bearing gifts of good Scotch whisky and homemade shortbread. The shortbread was added to the array of desserts on the sideboard, and she could bring to mind the ruby red of the cranberry jelly, and the cream on the trifle dotted with little slivers of green and orange peel. Jim and John Jo sat by the fire, while Ada and she put the finishing touches to the table. "You have such beautiful things Kate," Ada said, and indeed the table with its snowy damask cloth, glasses and silver cutlery shimmering in the light from the fire had looked lovely. Pat was playing some of the latest tunes popular in New York, and Jack and Louis were, she knew, deliciously tormented by the smells of roasting turkey coming from the kitchen.

"Are you not going to join me?" Kate heard Jim's disbelieving tones and John Jo's laughing rejoinder: "Maybe I've become a teetotaller Jim." "Go on outa that. You're pulling my leg." "I am but I'll not have anything just now, maybe a bit later."

She had been surprised because there was nothing John Jo liked better than a glass of good Scotch whisky, and she knew that he drank far too much of what was known locally as 'rotgut' out on the range. However, busy with the meal, she forgot about it but had noted at dinner that he ate little. "My stomach doesn't feel great Kate, I'll give it a bit of a rest. It will be fine in a few days," he had said, brushing aside her queries. Always a good host, he had been assiduous in topping up everybody's food and drink.

Afterwards, she remembered Pat sitting down at the old walnut piano, its woodwork glowing under the lamplight as he clipped some sheets of music to the slanting music rack. He had accompanied himself in songs he was to perform in a new show scheduled for the new year, and she could see how impressed Jim and Ada were with his talent. They had all been proud of him. "Give us a song yourself, John Jo," Ada had asked. "I'll give you a tune instead," and he had taken down his fiddle, but she could see that it had cost him an effort to do so. They finished the evening with a game of cards – whist, she recalled – John Jo had seemed to rally a little and they had been gay.

Over the next few months his health deteriorated rapidly. He lost his appetite, proclaiming himself full after the smallest of meals. He lost weight and began to suffer from pains in his abdomen. By early spring Kate had become seriously alarmed, but he refused to see Dr Miller holding to his belief that it was an infection that would pass. By late April, his skin and eyes were yellowing and she knew from her *Home Physician* that this was likely to be liver trouble. She had always feared this because of his heavy drinking and, unbeknownst to him, sent Jack to fetch Dr Miller.

John Jo was diagnosed with cirrhosis and possibly cancer of the liver and Dr Miller insisted that he needed hospital care. He was by this time in a fairly weakened state and reluctantly agreed. Arrangements were made to have him admitted to St Joseph's hospital in Denver. This was a Catholic hospital with an excellent reputation, and Kate wanted him to have the benefit of it's medical expertise as well as access to the comforts of his faith, because she had known then that he would not be returning home. She also made arrangements to go and lodge close by, to be with him. Hattie agreed to come and look after the boys and the ranch whilst she was away.

The few weeks they had together before the end were peaceful and curiously not unhappy. John Jo was weak but happy to have Kate there and, as always, she had been grateful for his need of her. This had always been his gift to her. She tried to explain once how much she valued his acknowledged need of her, how good it made her feel about herself, but he had just looked puzzled. "You are good, you don't need me to tell you that." And she remembered being glad that he had missed the point somehow.

During those weeks in hospital, Kate brought to mind for him some of their happiest times: "Remember how unsure Nan had been of you when you first came courting, John Jo? She was not too keen on men generally and certainly not if they took a drink, and you failed on both counts, and yet by the end of our first St John's Eve celebration, nothing was too good for you?" He had smiled. "Well, I think she knew that we both loved the old tunes and songs, and I suppose that was a bit of a bond."

But Kate knew that it was because he made her laugh, and there had been so little laughter in her life. She recalled him that night, insisting, "Come on Nan, we're going to show this crowd how to dance," and sweeping her into his arms, the pair of them had gone jigging around the garden until Nan, holding her sides from laughing and the tears streaming down her face, had begged him to stop. Kate laughed herself remembering it. "Oh, John Jo," she told him, "you made us all so merry. When I met you I felt alive. Remember, I had always been a bit cautious. You taught me to live, and you always wanted me." "That I have Kate," he said, "but I am afraid that I brought you some hard times too, and I thought I was going to give you a great life."

She told him that these things were in God's hands, and, that she was as grateful for the anguish as for the joys of her life, for it was the anguish, she said, that had led her closer to Our Lord.

They said little more then, but were at peace during those final days. Kate was holding his hand – then barely skin and bone – when he died on that late June morning in 1894. When they had covered his face for the last time, handsome and young again in death, she cried for their lost young love. But she was not anguished. He had earned his peace, and she could not wish him back to suffer more.

Pat, Jack and Louis all arrived in time for the requiem Mass, and seemed to her so absurdly young and sad with their black clothes and armbands. She remembered Louis' face had streaks where he had smudged it with his tears. A few of their closest friends from Casper made the long journey down for the funeral, but it had been a small band that followed the hearse to Mount Calvary. She glanced down at the energetic young city set against the backdrop of the mighty Rockies and noticed that the tips of Mt Evans were still covered in snow. She was glad of the little hollow covered in blue violets which were glinting in the sunshine beside the open grave, and hoped that these would spread to cover it. Pat led them all in singing *The Lord is my Shepherd* and the lovely words had comforted them as they listened to the lonely thud of the earth on the coffin.

Following John Jo's death, Kate turned her attention to her sons' welfare, with an urgency that suggested an awareness of the destiny that would take her from them. Solitude no longer held any terrors for her.

CHAPTER 10

The call to Cistercian life 1894-1897

"Before the mountains were brought forth, or ever thou hadst formed the earth and the world, even from everlasting to everlasting, thou art God."

Psalm 90 Vs. 2

The Cistercian Life requires solitude and community. Kate had learnt to love solitude, but struggled with communal living. Often, when preparing vegetables or engaged in some other task she strove to curb her irritation with a Sister's clumsiness or slowness. She had come to recognise the wisdom of St Benedict, in regarding the life of absolute solitude as befitting only a soul that has already attained perfection. Community had been necessary to her in order to learn patience, charity and humility.

WHAT HAD FINALLY decided her to become a Cistercian nun? Vincent's question had challenged Kate, and she struggled to explain how she had come to take such an astonishing step.

It had been seven or eight months after John Jo's death when she first spoke to Jack and Louis of her intentions. She was, she told Vincent, very sure by then that she was being called by God to closer communion with him in the contemplative life, and she wanted her boys to have time to come to terms with such a momentous decision.

Kate knew Pat to be content and settled into his life in New York, and that Vincent was securely provided for in Clare. She had written to Tom and Ellen to apprise them of her intentions, and to ask them to make the formal arrangements needed to secure his inheritance. She explained that she could not in conscience enter the priory until this had been done. They had understood her feelings as always, and did indeed take the required legal steps, so that she was easy in her mind about his future welfare.

She recalled the occasion well. It had been a dry sunny day following a spell of very cold weather, and the snow was drifting loosely over the hard ground when Jack and Louis returned in the late afternoon from an antelope hunt. They had set out in great glee when Jack's friend Tim Rowntree had stopped by with the news that a herd of antelope had been spotted south-west of Casper. Now they were back and Louis was very dejected while Jack looked resigned. "It was my fault Mam," Louis said, "I fired at the antelope when they were too far away to hit, I should have waited, Jack and Tim told me to hang fire but I thought I could hit them, and then they were off." "Yep" said Tim cheerily, "skimming away with the snow drifts, you need to work antelope real slow and easy, they're quick to scare."

All three quickly got over their disappointment as they tucked into the venison stew and mounds of buttery mashed potatoes and turnips Kate had prepared against their hunger. It was when they were having dessert that Tim turned to her and asked, "Do you ever think, Mrs Corbett, that you'd like to return to Ireland?" "Well Tim," she said, "what I would like now, would be to live a life of prayer and contemplation, and when I am sure that my lads here are secure and settled, I hope to do so within a Cistercian priory." Then, she had laughed, until the tears were streaming down her face, at the open mouthed expressions of utter astonishment on the three faces turned towards her!

She had dried her eyes and composed herself a little, when Louis said, "You're joking Mam," and this set her off again, and this time all joined in the laughter. She could not, she told Vincent, ever remember laughing so much, though she had no notion later why it had seemed so funny.

When they were eventually convinced that she was in earnest, Tim, who described himself as an agnostic, asked her a lot of questions about why she would want to do this. He listened very respectfully as she tried to convey the feelings of wonder and gratitude, the yearning towards God, which gave the contemplative life such a magnetic pull for her. She vividly recalled Louis' face as he listened, bemused, and struggled to understand. Jack had been quiet and a little in shock. His sadness and sense of loss would be the heaviest cross entailed in her decision.

Kate told Vincent a little about Tim, whose friendship with Jack had been such a comfort to her. For the most part Jack and Louis' companions were cowboys born of poor parents and, though skilled cattlemen and horsemen had little or no education. Tim had been very different. He was a graduate of Cambridge University and had come west with the Nebraska oil company for which Jack had also worked briefly as a guide. Their friendship dated from this time. Subsequently Tim was commissioned by a professor of one of the Boston colleges to collect fossils from the Badlands. A man of about thirty four, he had over the course of the previous seven or eight winters become a skilled hunter and trapper – the summer months were spent fossil hunting – and, surprisingly, a wonderful cook. Plump of face, with a receding hairline and warm humorous eyes, he and Jack had become close friends. Jack became a keen amateur fossil hunter himself and would, when free, join Tim in his hunt for specimens, and together they opened the eyes of Kate's imagination to a world she had not known existed. She became familiar with the terrifying birds and beasts that had stalked the earth: pterodactyls, iguanodons and dinosaurs of all sorts, not forgetting, as Jack reminded her, the tiny equines, barely four hands tall, from which our horses are probably descended.

They met other remarkable men, geologists working for the oil companies who unfolded the mysteries of the ancient world to them. She recalled the delicacy of spiral-shelled ammonite fossils, and the beautiful leaves, millions of years old, still delineated so clearly in the rock. However, it was only Tim who was to become a cherished part of the family. She believed that for him, too, they had been an oasis of comfort and civility which he valued.

Kate told her boys and Tim that evening that her journey to the contemplative life began with her childhood in Dublin. She described how the life of the Church nourished her senses by its warmth and colour and the stimulation and pageantry of its liturgy. She spoke of an ideal of selfless love which it held aloft and how her childish steps were set on a path of prayer and self denial which she believed helped her to stay within the orbit of that love. Of course she had strayed from it frequently, but had been led back again and again, through the patient guidance and sacraments of the Church. It was little wonder, she said, that she had a profound gratitude for its wisdom and care. Kate felt her world to have been charged with the presence of God, and the supernatural was as familiar to her as the air she breathed. She regarded their daily life and habits as having been blessed by the requirements of the faith, as they thanked God for the new day and the old, for their meals, even for the disappointments that drew them closer to Christ in suffering.

Kate was aware that many of the practices of the Church, such as devotions to the saints, or to our Blessed Virgin, or pilgrimages to holy shrines, were seen by very many people as superstitions, and while she did not hold many of these practices as essential to the life of grace, she did not see them as harmful either, and indeed at best, she believed that they could open the soul to an easy acceptance of the supernatural. Kate regarded the almost exclusive reliance on human reason that had come to characterise the age in which they lived, as restrictive, not only to the human spirit but also to the imagination and the heart.

She greatly missed the support of the Church's liturgy when she went to Wyoming, and had struggled to maintain the practice of the faith. She had been rigorous about nightly recitation of the rosary, which encouraged them, she told Vincent, to reflect on the mysteries of the incarnation. However, cut off from direct participation in the cycle of the Church's liturgical life Kate had felt the deprivation acutely. She relied on spiritual reading and meditation and had come to know the old and new Testaments very well. In this she was helped greatly by the guidance of a Benedictine priest, whom she had met in Buffalo, and with whom she was to correspond for over a decade, as he became her spiritual advisor.

Fr. Mulholland had been a quiet, frail man, who spoke to her on one of the many occasions when she sought refuge in the cathedral in Buffalo, and to whom she told her sorrows. She remembered that he had just listened and did not offer any advice, but said that he would pray for her. This holy man brought her healing through listening, and had been the channel, she believed, through which God poured so much grace into her life.

Kate recalled the joy of that first celebration of Mass in Casper – still without a church, at that time. She could bring every detail so vividly to mind. It had been in the late summer of 1890, shortly after Wyoming attained its statehood. William Dunn, their first representative to the state legislature and a devout Catholic, had prevailed upon his friend, Father Francis Nugent, to make the journey from Cheyenne to baptise his little son Eugene and celebrate Mass in the town hall. She conveyed the exhilaration and joy with which they transformed the plain old hall into a sanctuary, as worthy as they could make it, of welcoming the Lord. Her heart had been full, she said, as she watched the light play over her beautiful damask cloth which covered the table that was to serve as an altar, and which was adorned with the red and white roses William brought back with him from Cheyenne.

Introibo ad altare Dei, the Mass had begun. Kate described the increasing quiet as the moving ritual, against all the odds of individual, wayward inclinations, quietened their restless spirits. It was with one voice that they responded to the call, *Sursum Corda – Habemus ad Dominum*, as they moved towards the profound stillness of the Consecration . She spoke of her gratitude then for "the gift of a Divine Love knowable only through Faith," and regretted that such knowledge was increasingly dismissed at that time, and the riches it contained discarded. She recalled the sense of peace that permeated that little assembly following Father Nugent's dismissal: *Dominus vobiscum; Ite missa est.* She prayed that they would all cherish and nourish their faith, which she regarded as the greatest blessing with which they had been gifted.

They had periodic visits from Father Nugent over the years, usually when a child was born requiring baptism, when he would say Mass either in the town hall or the Episcopal church, and sometimes in the Trevetts' or Dunns' homes, where there was enough room. These celebrations had always been a source of joy and renewal, and were also enjoyed as social occasions. For Kate it was never enough; she thirsted for full and frequent participation in the great cycle of the Church's prayer, and those tantalisingly rare events stoked as much as slaked her thirst.

She tried to explain this to Jack, when he had asked her, "Can you not be close to God out here, Mam, amid all this grandeur and solitude?" The occasion had been a very happy time, some eighteen months before she left, when Jack and Tim took her on a wonderful trip up into Big Horn country. It had been her first and indeed only camping trip. It was a magical time. That first evening as they drove into the violet shadows between the hills, she saw a great wolf outlined against the setting sun, standing motionless on a ridge away to her left. The glorious crimson and amber sky gave way to dull grey by the time they had set up camp. The boys made a comfortable bed for her in the wagon, and built a roaring fire as the night had been chilly. They roasted potatoes in the embers, which they ate with slices of bacon washed down with excellent coffee, and my, were they hungry? Kate could not remember food ever tasting as good as it did then. The boys shot sage chicken and jack rabbit, which they skinned and dressed in the evenings in readiness for the following day. Tim had brought with him some wonderful pickled trout while she baked biscuits on a griddle over the camp fire. Tim cooked a porcupine one night, which she did not think she could eat, she told Vincent, but indeed she did and enjoyed it.

The nights had been best, the skies alive with stars and a silence only deepened by the faint moaning of the pines and aspens all around them. The solitude was accentuated most nights by the wailing of the coyotes or the lonely howl of the wolf, and one evening one had trotted nonchalantly right by the wagon.

"I do feel close to God here, who could fail to see his face amidst such splendour?" Kate said in reply to Jack's question. "You know that the first monks read the earth not just as the work but as the Word of God." Its beauty and mystery seemed so sacred to her, and it was this, as well as her increasing appetite for solitude, that drew her to the Cistercian way of life. In the beginning she was frightened by the depth of silence that had surrounded her – a silence that seemed to stretch into eternity. In those early days, empty and alone, she spoke of learning "to listen to God," and found it easier to pray and meditate. She began to shake off the noise of the world a little, she said, and to rid herself of the more futile preoccupations and worries with which she had wasted her time. The silence helped to make more space for God in her life, and she came not only to need it, but to long for an even deeper silence.

Kate and Jack were both a little emotional following this conversation and they did not say much more, but little by little Jack came to accept and to understand her decision. Of course, while John Jo was alive, and Jack and Louis still young and in need of her, she had not considered the possibility of entering a religious order. Indeed, she came to think of marriage and parenthood as her apprenticeship in learning to love, just as she saw the monastic life, to use St Benedict's words, as her final "school in love". She regarded herself humorously as a poor student, believing that they had all suffered because of her shortcomings. It was with real remorse that she remembered the many periods of bad humour, peevishness, self-absorption and nagging criticism that she had visited upon John Jo. Yet he, who never thought of himself as particularly good or holy, had, she told Vincent, always been forgiving. She had no doubt that Christ, who promised, "Blessed be the merciful, for they shall obtain mercy," had forgiven him his failures too.

It took the savage deaths of both her little girls to open her eyes, to the depth of self love entailed in the passionate protective feelings she had for all of her beloved children. She had thought this love to be selfless, but learnt through suffering the extent to which her own needs were bound up with her feelings. However, the depth of those feelings led her, she said, to an appreciation of, and trust in, the love of her heavenly Father. The aching vacuum left by their deaths marked the beginning of the real reign of Christ in her heart. She turned to Him as He had asked "Come to me all you who labour and are burdened" and over the years, she believed that He had indeed refreshed her, so that in truth, her little girls had drawn her with them into an eternal timescape. There had been anguish too at the parting from her beautiful little boy. She had tried to be glad for him, knowing the value of the prospects offered, and had indeed become so. Although it was a hard school in which to learn about love, she would not, she said, have had it otherwise, and indeed she thanked God for it.

After John Jo's death, the call to live more closely with those who love God became more insistent. Kate was acutely aware of the gift of time and of the need to put it to good use. She had a profound sense of the world's need of Grace. The previous decade in Wyoming had disclosed to her, she said, the depths to which men and women could sink, without His guidance. Hundreds if not thousands of men swarmed around them during that time, in a frenzied search for gold and other precious metals. Kate thought it pitiable, to see the spiritual poverty reflected in the degraded and profane way so many of these men lived, and even sadder to watch the poor women who followed them. They had so little sense of the enormous worth that, she believed, God wanted to confer on them, or of their value as human beings made in His likeness.

Among the most influential books sent to her by Father Mulholland was the very succinct *Rule of St Benedict*. This refreshingly practical guide to living a communal life, devoted to the love of God and our neighbour, had been a revelation to Kate. It conveyed an acceptance of human frailty, and the robust balance it recommended between prayer, work, silence and worship, spoke to her very directly. The intention gradually formed and strengthened in her to use her remaining years to become more fully a follower of Christ, within what she regarded as the wise guidance of this holy rule.

She met and secured the support of their local Bishop for her intentions, and began to correspond with the Reverend Mother at Stapehill in Dorset, as there was no Cistercian convent in Ireland at that time. Kate had some money which had been left to her by her mother when she died, and without which her entry to the priory might have been too much of a liability, given her age and the dire poverty of the sisters. John Jo had insisted that this was to be kept for her support in the event of his death.

It was to be two more years before she made the long journey back across the atlantic to Dorset, and entered the priory in Stapehill. During that time she had been able to help Louis and Jack file for additional land, and successfully applied for permission to dig irrigation channels. They also applied for naturalistion and secured citizenship. Most importantly, it gave Jack and Louis time to become reconciled to her decision. Louis had by this time met Nellie, who was to become his wife and this, of course, greatly cushioned him against her loss. It was harder for Jack.

Kate vividly recalled their last Christmas together. Pat had come down from New York, and Jim and Ada Roche as well as Tim joined them for the celebration. They were all, she remembered, a little constrained, conscious of this being their final one together. After the meal they tucked into some delicious chocolates, ordered – as were all their provisions then – through a catalogue and delivered by Jed the mail carrier. Pat did not feel like playing his usual party music, and indeed, it would not have been right just then. Tim surprised them all by asking, "Would you like me to give you a bit of old Bach?" They had not known he was interested in music, and of course assented. He was a very accomplished musician, and his piano recital that night of the music from *St Matthew's Passion* was extraordinarily moving. It brought them to a place of quiet and hope and it had been a good way to end that Christmas.

Kate was up early on that last morning and wandered outside to watch the day begin to lighten. The mysterious notched façade of Mt Casper revealed itself as the early morning light threw the gullies into relief. She had been acutely aware of all the familiar sounds, the chickens rustling in their coop, the repeated cry of the cockerel and the calves beginning to bawl their hunger. She recalled Jack's collie, Jake, nestling into her hand, and found herself beginning to feel a little tearful. She did not linger.

She had disposed of most of her personal belongings before that final morning, and was left with one small suitcase, containing all she would need for the remaining few weeks before she entered the priory. Louis had gone to get the buggy ready, and Jack came into her room to fetch her case. She showed him the casket of jewellery that she was leaving for the girls that he and Louis would one day marry, before replacing it in the drawer of the otherwise empty chest. The room had looked so bleak, cleared now of all her clutter, and it was this, she thought, that finally triggered the tearing sobs that poor

Jack had held in check for so long. Indeed she was glad of them, she held him in her arms and stroked his hair as she had not done since he was a little boy, and she cried with him. It had been good for both of them, and they were all three able to say goodbye at the station with just a few tears.

Vincent himself could recall how peaceful were those final weeks that Kate had spent with him in Quin on her way to Dorset. They had helped, she said, to soothe the raw wound left by the memory of Jack's pain and courage, and she had added, characteristically, "God's will be done."

CHAPTER 11

Holy Cross Priory, Stapehill, Dorset. January 1909

"As for man, his days are as grass: as a flower of the field, so he flourisheth. For the wind passeth over it, and it is gone; and the place thereof shall know it no more."

Psalm 103 Vs. 15 & 16

ELEVEN YEARS had passed since that first visit to Holy Cross Priory. It was with a great deal more comfort that Vincent regarded the parlour on what was to be his final visit to Kate that wet October afternoon in 1909. Now infused with the interest and good will of a community of women to whom he was uniquely linked, it felt warm and welcoming. He tucked into the hot tea, fresh scones and delicious strawberry jam served by Sister Gregory, a fellow countrywoman of whom Kate, he knew, was very fond.

She had spoken to him of the loneliness of Gregory's journey within monastic life. She was different from her English sisters, whose cast of mind had been formed to some extent by the more rational protestant culture within which they lived, despite their adherence to the old faith. Gregory on the other hand, had acquired an innocent familiarity with the mystical, through her immersion in the life of a Church dominated by a faith, and set of traditional beliefs that, Kate believed, contained profound truths, but owed less to rational thought. Gregory liked to make novenas and had great trust in the power attaching to relics which seemed to some of the sisters to border on the superstitious, and so she had been a little alien. She had been able to bear her loneliness, Kate said, and it was good to have seen this eased over the years, as her sisters gradually came to accept, and indeed, appreciate, the essential goodness of this big nun, whom she believed to be very close to God.

Vincent had been apprised of Kate's illness by Reverend Mother, but was still taken aback to hear her slow hesitant steps making their way to the little grilled panel. He was aware of Sister Gregory easing her on to a chair and sensed her smiling as she thanked her slightly awkward fellow country-woman. He knew that she found Gregory's practical and common sense approach to suffering a comfort, and that she did not need to cushion her from its impact.

It had been a good morning, Kate said in response to his query, with no sign of the nausea that was by then her frequent companion. She had been able to savour the simple breakfast, her pleasure made greater, she told Vincent, by the relief on the face of Sister Veronica. This kindly anxious Sister had been assigned to nurse her and Kate knew that her difficulty in finding any appetite, even when not nauseous, was a sore trial for her. She, who used to have such a zest for food!

The memories of those distant Thanksgiving dinners with John Jo and the boys no longer had power to disturb her. What a torment they had been during her early years when, tired and hungry, after an afternoon's work in the priory garden, she sat down with her sisters to a glass of milk and a slice of bread, or sometimes a bowl of stewed apples from the garden. How often the image of those festive meals came to taunt her. She asked God's forgiveness for the times when she gave free reign to her memory and imagination. She would smell again the aroma of roast turkey crackling, briefly retrieved from the oven to insert the potatoes and parsnips for roasting. She could see in her mind's eye the table sparkling with snowy linen, the glass and cutlery reflected in the sideboard mirror alongside the apple and squash pies and the poached pears.

More potent still, had been the images of John Jo and the boys - John Jo with his stiff leg extended, resting on the fender and fencing in the odd escaping log while discussing with Jack plans for draining the marshy land in the lower back field. Kate would smile at the memory of Jack's energetic optimism, glad of its ability to sustain John Jo, then beginning to struggle with the weariness that would grow heavier over the years. Pat as usual would be tinkling away at the piano, absorbed in yet another tune he had unearthed. Pat had known everyone in their neighbourhood and beyond, and all had seemed happy to pause and dredge up songs and tunes almost forgotten in the grind of their daily toil, their own pleasure renewed by his delight. There was Louis, always starving, and fairly dancing with anticipation in front of the fire, while he tried to interest Pat in a blow by blow account of the game of handball, he had been playing.

So faint and benign now were those memories that had been such a torment then. How she had ached to retrieve the enfolding warmth and comfort of the wholesome joys of family life, and how bleak and unlovely – even inhuman - were the monastic walls that surrounded her. It was, she believed, only by God's grace that she was still there, when faith and conviction felt so thin and inadequate. How little and fragile her soul had been when such pleasures held her in thrall!

The faint echo of the chant drifting from the Chapel reminded Kate of the consolation she had found in the singing of the Divine Office. It brought with it an exhilarating and profoundly satisfying sense of peace which was undoubtedly, she told Vincent, one of God's greatest gifts to her in monastic life.

It had been so ever since that first Thursday evening, when she arrived at the Abbey exhausted and drained by the journey and the terrible finality of her decision. She had been brought straight to the chapel for Benediction where the beautiful strains of the *Tantum Ergo* soothed her pain and desperate loneliness. A sense of the awfulness of what she had done came to her like a recurring hammer blow during that first year, leaving her in its wake, almost physically sick and weak. The bemused images of Louis and Nellie – their bewilderment that she would not be with them for Thanksgiving or Christmas - would come unbidden. It was however the stoic pain on Jack's face that had haunted Kate with most anguish during those early months.

She had needed God's Grace, she said, and He gave it to her - hour after hour and day after day, as she immersed herself in the liturgical round of prayer and meditation. It never failed to bring ease to the torment that raged within her, though she continued to suffer long periods when her state of mind remained numb and arid, visited by doubts about her vocation. The sense of being cut off, virtually dead to her dearly loved family, had been an acute aching wound, and the sharpness of the pain threatened at times to overwhelm her. Why had she chosen this path? How could God be so cruel as to ask this of her? ... of her family?

It had been the warm, sure rise of the Gregorian chant, murmuring psalms of praise and thanks, filling the church and her soul with the solace and certitude of His love that brought her the reassurance and conviction she needed. Kate particularly loved the night office. The bells would call them from sleep around two am, and in that dark hour they would straighten the habits in which they had lain down fully clothed, grope for their shoes, and make their way through the shadows to the Chapel. She described how the deep silence, and the peace and holiness of the night would enfold them, as they filled the darkness with the wonderful psalms of Matins and Lauds, making holy the hours of the night. Later on at Prime and Tierce, the Church would begin to fill with light, and they were there to receive the giftedness of the new day. So would the whole day be made holy, by the chanting of the Divine Office at regulated intervals, until the close of day brought them to Compline, the evening prayer of the Church.

It had taken some time for this profoundly satisfying round of prayer and silence, which was the pulse of her new monastic life, to bring the peace and solace which Kate so craved during those early months, but it did, and she had grown to love the spiritual waters within which she was slowly learning to swim. Kate thanked God, she told Vincent, for the suffering which taught her the detachment necessary to let Him in. He did not take away the acute pain she felt at being so separate from her beloved family, but she became able to bear this cross, and even to be thankful, that she could share more fully in His suffering by so doing.

The requirement of the Benedictine Rule that they labour physically to provide for their own wants, had also helped to soothe Kate's pain. She delighted in being sent to work in the garden. Looking down over the still valley of the Stour, its water meadows so often delicately gauzed in mist during those early mornings, she would dig and weed with gusto feeling very close then to her boys, no doubt similarly labouring in Wyoming and Clare. She would ask the Lord to keep them close and watch over them.

Kate had spoken of the sisters' care of her in her illness, admitting wryly that devotion could be tiring, and she had to struggle at times to give it the reassurance it called for. Reverend Mother came to see her in the infirmary every morning after Chapter when the day's duties were allocated. She had smiled, aware of how much she loved this woman, whose strength and faith had comforted her during some of her harshest trials. She recalled the day less than two years after her profession. She had been in the garden gathering up leaves and dead foliage, when the new postulant Maria came to ask her to report to Mother. Surprised, she took off her gardening apron, washed her hands and knocked on that well known door. Mother was standing by the door as if she had been waiting for the knock, her normally serene almost impassive countenance taut and pale. Kate remembered being surprised when she led her to two chairs in the middle of the room; usually she remained behind her desk, where she would listen patiently to their recital of failings, and counsel them with wisdom and – were they inclined to take themselves too seriously – some wit.

Then she told her quietly and simply and Kate felt the blood drain from her face. She had found herself swaying on the seat and Mother held her as she slowly absorbed the fact that her Pat was dead. Louis had sent a telegram stating that Pat, weakened by pneumonia, had died just hours before he was to play the lead role in a drama opening that night in New York. The event had been a charitable one, organised to raise funds for poor Irish immigrants. He died almost immediately. There was a medical doctor in the audience but there had been nothing he could do and Pat received the Last Rites from the hands of one of the priests who had helped organise the show.

Dreamy, impish, fun-loving Pat, who alone of her boys seemed to accept her decision to enter the Cistercian priory without resentment, or indeed pain. He had been an unusually happy child who had grown into a sociable young man, popular with friends and family for his ready sense of gaiety and love of fun. There had however, been a darker, melancholic side to Pat's character which had emerged during those early months in Wyoming, and there were long periods when he had been withdrawn and hard to reach. It was an immense comfort to her, to have found him in so equable a state of mind and at ease with himself during her final visit to New York. When she ventured to enquire about this, he spoke simply about the waves of blackness that he had been subject to since mid-adolescence, and which he now regarded as his cross for life. When struggling with these visitations it was not possible, he said, to be available to anyone and for this reason he did not believe he should ever marry or have children.

Kate had cried then for the loneliness of the road before him, and for the dignity and patience with which he described "the dead weight" his life became for him during these times. The tautness of the lines around his eyes and mouth bore eloquent testament to a suffering normally masked by gaiety and cheer. He spoke of a close friend, James McCoy, in whom he could confide, and who was a "rock" at such times. For the rest, he said, it was the routine of work and social obligations that got him through. She was glad to know that he had found increasing comfort in his faith and went to Mass and communion regularly at St Patrick's Cathedral.

He was insistent, during that last visit, that he was enjoying a great spell and refused to dwell further on his trials. He was genuinely interested in her decision and the reasons for it, and wonderfully free of any sense of loss and pain for himself. This had been such a comfort to Kate and they had a very happy time. They reminisced about their shared love of music and singing, going back over the standard tunes and songs she had taught him. He had wondered, he said, at her reluctance to sing and play, other than what was needed to illustrate what she was teaching him, when she so clearly loved and was moved by music, and could play so well.

Kate had explained as best she could. Her first intimation of the lure of the spiritual life happened when she was just seventeen. During the course of the three day retreat in her final year at school she had been inspired by the passion and conviction of the tall, rather plain Redemptorist missionary, who had conjured up for them such a luminous image of the life of Grace – "the interior mystical life in which God invites us to share." Her own life seemed so messy by comparison - strange feelings, confusing thoughts and the vast uncharted expanse of the future to fill. She longed to embrace this pure and simple path, and remembered well the feeling of relief that washed over her as she contemplated her future as a nun. Perhaps because she was so young, the span of a human life seemed infinitesimal, compared to that eternal life to which she thought she was being called.

Pat smiled at what had been her youthful enthusiasm, as she spoke about her longing at that time to "melt my life into that of the Living Christ" – a phrase of the Missionary's that had lodged deeply in her romantic soul. She knew that she would have to pray and make sacrifices, and was determined to deny her own wishes and desires as they had been admonished, in order to make way for the seeds of supernatural life. The missionary impressed upon them the danger of being imprisoned by their own pleasures and wishes. Kate decided then that, since music, and singing was one of her greatest pleasures, she would only sing and play when required to, in the service of God, or by some other duty. This initial dash for the ascetic heights had dwindled away over the years, and it was only after the deaths of her beloved girls that she reclaimed her resolution. Indeed, there had been no virtue in this, she said, as she had little inclination to make music for a long number of years. The anaesthetising round of duty and family life had gradually drawn a thin film of protection over the raw wounds of this most terrible loss, but it was Pat, with his love of music and songs who helped her achieve a deeper healing. Her delight in helping him explore and develop his undoubted talent for music heralded the return of a sense of joy to the home. By then her soul had been ploughed, she said, by the sorrow and toil of the preceding years and was stronger. She had been able to remain steadfast in confining her own love for music to the service of Pat's development. Kate was surprised by the warmth of the hug Pat gave her following this explanation.

These thoughts and memories drifted past her numbed mind, as Reverend Mother held her on that autumn afternoon. Again, a dreary sense of the futility of her vocation washed over her. Why had she not offered him more support, been available to comfort him when she had him? Mother led her into the Chapel where she knelt down beside her. "We will pray the Rosary for the repose of Pat's soul," she said and Kate remembered being dully surprised by her choice of the glorious rather than the sorrowful mysteries, but had responded bleakly to the hypnotic round of the beads.

She spoke of God's mercy in granting her then a very great grace, which had filled her soul with peace and even joy. She had been visited by a sense of certainty, that Pat was happy and at peace with God. This certitude was of the order of knowledge rather than hope or faith, she said, and described herself as having a physical awareness of Pat "being held in the palm of God's hand." Kate was not given to melodramatic imagery, but this was the only way she could convey the reality of the experience she had. She held this to be true, with a conviction greater than any natural certainty she had ever experienced, and was in no doubt that she had been granted a mystical experience. It was to be the only one of her life, and she remained grateful that it was granted to her when she most needed it. For a week or perhaps two, Kate remained suffused with an extraordinary sense of joy and peace, as she prayed for Pat night and day.

Poor Mother had been troubled by what must have felt like an unnaturally ineffable calm, and she feared for Kate's mental health. When Kate spoke to her about this experience, she remained cautious, warning her that her mood might shift back to the earlier despairing bleakness. However this had not happened and while that vivid, almost physical, knowledge faded gradually, she never forgot what she believed to have been God's great gift of consolation to her. The memory of this experience continued to support her throughout her monastic life, and the sense of peace and joy it generated had always remained at some profound level, even when overlain at times with troubles of one kind or another.

Kate told Vincent of the kindness with which Reverend Mother had remained on spiritual watch for her over so many years. It was not long after Pat's death when she asked her to assume the duty of organist to the community. She knew of course of her earlier sacrifice, and became the instrument of God's generous care of her in giving back, enriched, the gift she had made to Him.

From then on, Kate would accompany the sisters' chant of the Divine Office throughout all the hours. The struggle to maintain pace and tone had been a challenge but this was more than compensated for by the pleasure she gleaned from the music she loved. She was always last to leave the chapel, while it still resonated with the sublime roll of the chant, it's austere simplicity warmed by the soft glow of the early morning light, and she had known an almost sensual delight, certainly greater than those of the flesh which had once been so familiar to her.

Kate worried about the joyful sense of exhilaration with which she used to look forward to, even the practice, of the Liturgy. Mother had laughed out loud when she confessed her scruples, querying why she should think that God did not intend us to experience such pleasure? How she had helped Kate to know the gladness of her vocation. She would speak about religious life as "a school in which we learn from God how to be happy ... how to enjoy what is good and beautiful in life while always on the alert to ensure that the will remains dedicated to God".

Free of scruples then, Kate revelled in being central to the making of that sublime music inspired by the Church's cycle of prayer, Gregorian chant. For such a treasure it had been easy to forgo the pleasures of the wonderful, impassioned music of Bach, Beethoven and Monteverdi, as required by St Benedict's rule. She had been allowed, she believed, to play and chant her way into a deeper faith and an ever greater sense of peace and gladness. For this she was very thankful.

Kate was tired by the end of that last visit when Sister Gregory came to help her back to the infirmary, and with characteristic practical kindness waited until she had said her goodbyes to her beloved son before easing her upright.

..."Goodbye dear, dear Vincey. May God Bless you and keep you always."

These were to be the last words Kate spoke to him. She died on the seventh of February 1910.

RIP

The Pursuit of Kate Corbett

Epilogue

When I was about eleven, the story of my great-grandmother's life laid siege to my imagination, and it has never loosened its grip. It seemed to me then a truly epic story, and it still does today. She was baptised Katherine Mary Agnes O'Toole, but was known for most of her life as Kate Corbett.

Born in Victorian Dublin in 1841, her family was one of the rising Catholic bourgeoisie of that city. The bulk of the aristocracy had abandoned Dublin after the union of the two Parliaments in 1800, and into their place moved the rising Catholic professional and business classes. She belonged to the latter, and grew up in a lovely home in St Stephen's Green in the heart of Georgian Dublin.

She married the second son of a substantial tenant farmer from Co. Clare, John Jo Corbett. He worked in the Civil Service in Dublin, which was, of course, then part of the British Empire. The coming of Catholic Emancipation in 1829 had opened up such posts to educated Catholics.

Dublin, then as now, was a convivial city, where good company and witty conversation was always on offer (at least for men) in its many public houses. John Jo enjoyed a drink in good company, and Kate worried about this. In addition, her parents would very likely have been concerned about the rising tide of Fenianism in the city at that time, and its lure for young men of John Jo's class and background. She encouraged him to transfer to the Indian Civil Service where he would be removed from this allure. The proposal appealed to John Jo's sense of adventure and he duly went to India.

After some years, he moved out of the Empire's employment to become involved in tea planting. I imagine that life within the Raj, or indeed any part of the British Civil Service, was less than congenial to one of his background. During those post-famine years Ireland was in the grip of a land war, characterised at times by acts of violence and terror which shocked the British. A Catholic of John Jo's farming background, from a part of the country where there had been considerable agrarian disturbance even before the Famine, is likely to have been regarded with considerable wariness. This must have been oppressive, I imagine, to someone of his convivial spirit.

Following a number of successful years in tea planting, John Jo left to take up a post as a big game hunter. This post was likely to have been sponsored by a group of tea planters, concerned about the risk posed to livestock and even villagers by dangerous animals

Kate's father died in 1866, and John Jo returned to Dublin, where they married in 1869. Surprisingly, he resumed working for the Civil Service. Perhaps the general political climate had become more welcoming for Catholics, or his reputation and ability had been established as beyond reproach

They set up home in Blackrock, and went on to have six children in fairly quick succession, four boys and two girls, of whom my grandfather, Vincent Corbett, was the youngest. The relentless round of domestic and office life must have been hard on John Jo. At any rate, he gradually succumbed to the lure of the pub with its promise of conviviality, and his drinking became again a matter of concern for Kate.

They had become aware of the opportunities opening up in the US for migrants of education and ability, and she was glad to nourish John Jo's interest in this. The upshot was that they sailed for New York in September 1884 with their three youngest children. Vincent was aged five, Kath seven and Edith nine. The others were left, (in the care of Kate's mother and sister Elisa, I assume), to finish out the school year and free their parents to prepare a home in the New World.

Kath died of diphtheria on the boat on the way out to the US and Edith died not long after their arrival in New York. There, in upper New York State, John Jo took up a post with a company selling farming equipment. They quickly became aware of the opportunities available for the acquisition of land under the provisions of the Homesteading legislation. John Jo was keen to avail of this and Kate agreed, and so it was that they came to settle in Casper, Wyoming.

John Jo's brother Tom was a substantial tenant farmer in Clare. He had no children of his own, and with his wife Ellen offered to raise one of theirs, with a view to their inheriting the farm. This was a time when the strong farming class to which Tom belonged, was extending and securing its hold over the land in Ireland. Agricultural profits were good, and a rural bourgeoisie of "near gentry" status was emerging in the countryside. The prospects for whichever son was chosen would have been very bright.

Initially the choice fell upon their third son, Louis. However, he could not settle, so it was decided that my grandfather, the youngest in the family should be sent. Aged barely eight, and labelled, he was sent on his own from Casper in Wyoming to the village of Quin in county Clare in Ireland. He travelled by train to Chicago, and thence to New York where he took a boat for Queenstown in Cork. There, he was met by Ellen, Tom and Louis and returned with them to Quin. He grew up on the farm, returning periodically to visit his family in Wyoming.

In 1894 John Jo died of liver cancer in St Joseph's Catholic hospital in Denver, Colorado. Following his death Kate filed for additional land for Jack and Louis and also applied for permission to have the land irrigated. In addition she and both boys completed their naturalisation applications and were in due course granted citizenship. She also wrote to Tom to ask that legal arrangements to secure Vincent's inheritance be put in place, and this was duly done.

In 1897 at the age of fifty seven, Kate, having provided for their futures, said goodbye to her sons. She sailed for Cork and made her way to Quin to spend a few weeks with Vincent before going to Dublin to say goodbye to her sister Elisa. From there, she took the boat from Kingstown to Holyhead, and found her way to the little village of Staples in Dorset. Here, she entered a Cistercian Priory and, two and a half years later, was professed a Cistercian nun. She died at the age of seventy and was laid to rest wrapped in the cowl of her Cistercian habit and uncoffined, as was then the custom of the order. Sister Veronica wrote a very moving account of her death and last days to Vincent in Clare.

Four years after entering the abbey she received news of the sudden death of her first born son Pat. He was an actor and musician and died of pneumonia just hours before he was due to go on stage in the lead role of a show in New York

The one tragedy Kate was spared was a knowledge of the murder of her beloved Jack. He was shot in 1920 at the age of forty six by a young ranch hand of whose criminal record he had been unaware when employing him just a week beforehand. By then he was a highly respected and substantial ranch owner, and my grandfather was to inherit half his legacy.

Vincent visited Kate faithfully once a year from the time she entered the priory until her death in February 1910. He in turn relayed the story of her life to my mother from whom I was to hear it. Vincent himself became a highly respected and unusually scholarly farmer in Clare, whose reputation was to survive well into the 1970s when I went to work in west Clare as its first professional social worker. I derived great credibility from my status as Vincent Corbett's granddaughter which helped to offset the more dubious status attached to being a professional social worker.

This story is based on an amalgam of archival material – birth, marriage and death certificates, old newspaper texts, street directories, ship's manifestos and other documents, together with information provided by my mother, Margaret Mary Corbett, and my uncle Rev. Jack Corbett CSSR (Kate's grandchildren). It was with great regret that I read in Sister Veronica's letter to my grandfather after her death, that she had burnt all Kate's letters as she had asked her to do. They would surely have told us so much more. In my attempt to bring her story to life, descriptions of the political, social and cultural circumstances with which her life was intertwined, are based on real events. The characters of the family members, though hinted at by some family lore, are drawn from imagination, as are the relationships between them, and of course the range of minor characters introduced are purely fictional. However, by rooting these in the real circumstances of period and place, I hope to have given them a measure of credibility. For those wishing to disentangle fact and fiction, I have provided an appendix clarifying the sources of the information for the different chapters.

The Boy who came back.

My Grandparents Vincent and Mary Corbett
with their two daughters Kitty and Margaret
Mary circa 1917.

Vincent Corbett with his wife Mary, and daughters Kitty and Margaret Mary circa 1916, in front of the home he was to inherit from his Uncle Tom and Aunt Ellen by whom he was raised from the age of eight.

Appendix

Chapters [1,2 3 & 4]

In building up a picture of Kate and John Jo's lives, I relied not only on records, such as birth, death and marriage certificates, but also on censuses, Griffiths valuation returns, Thom's and Slater's directories, newspaper texts and other documentation. I drew heavily on local and national historical research. Among many useful books, R K Foster's *History of Modern Ireland*, alongside some more idiosyncratic local works, e.g. *Diary of an Irish Countryman,* proved invaluable in building up a picture of what shaped life in Ireland, and more specifically, in Clare and Dublin, during that period. I am also indebted to some excellent fictional writing, and particularly that of Kate O'Brien, for honing my sense of Irish, middle-class, religious sensibility at that time.

Family lore, suggesting that Kate and John Jo went to India together, was refuted by the records of their marriage in 1869, and the births of their six children between 1871 and 1879, all of which took place in Dublin. They most certainly would not have gone unmarried, and John Jo's youth at the time would lend credence to my account. My mother (Margaret Mary Corbett) always told me that Kate encouraged him to go, so that he would "get away from his cronies", whom she considered a bad influence. Interestingly, my Uncle Jack (Rev. Jack Corbett CSSR) said that he went, "because he found the Deeds of Registry office deathly tame". My story accommodates both perspectives.

A Dr Corbett did indeed live near them in St Stephen's Green, but whether he was any relation of Father Dan or John Jo I do not know. Father Dan Corbett was the priest who married Kate and John Jo and was almost certainly a relative. He was a parish priest in Quin.

I drew particularly on the scholarly work of William Dalrymple on India in the nineteenth century, some autobiographical material by Rumer Godden, and Charles Allen's biography of Rudyard Kipling, alongside some internet research into tea planting, to build up a picture of what life might have been like for John Jo there. The account of the shooting of the tiger is almost verbatim as told to me by my uncle Jack shortly before he died. I like to think that it was as my grandfather would have heard it from John Jo on one of his visits to Wyoming. However a version of this story told to my sister Gemma by Uncle Jack when he was a lot younger suggests that the Corbett responsible for the killing of the tiger was a different Corbett and not a family relative. In giving preference to the more romantic version as told to me directly I may be accused of a lesser degree of objectivity as by then Uncle Jack was a lot older and arguably less clear in his mind.

Chapter 5

A rather sprawling trawl of the web yielded some help here, as did some excellent literature about the reality of life for Irish emigrants in the north east of the United States, and the structure and influence of the Catholic Church. Notable among my many sources of help was the work of Burrows and Wallace, *Gotham – a history of New York City 1898,* John Brinnin's *The Sway of the Grand Saloon,* and *Inventing Irish America* by Tim Meagher. Though family lore stated that both little girls died on the voyage over, records confirm that Edie did, in fact, arrive in New York, hence, my assumption that she died shortly after her arrival.

Chapters [6,7, 8, 9 & 10]

For these chapters I drew on innumerable sources of information. I need however to single out those upon which I relied heavily to try and picture what it must have been like to live in Wyoming in the late nineteenth century. A J Mokler's *History of Natrona County* was invaluable, as were those first-hand accounts contained in *Letters from a Woman Homesteader*, *A Lady's life in the Rockies*, *Red Walls and Homesteads* and John McPhee's *Rising from the Plains*.

Much of the factual information based on archival material was unearthed for us in Casper by local genealogist Roddy Burwell. This was supplemented by Carl Hallberg and Cindy Brown (Wyoming State Archivists) and Kevin Anderson (Western History Archivist attached to Casper College). Amongst other useful information they drew our attention to the story of Jack's discovery of the local mummy, and the advertisement in the *Casper Weekly Mail* of June 1889 announcing that J J Corbett was opening for business as a land agent. It was Roddy too who helped us to identify the exact location of where the ranch had been, and with the help of the McMurray family we were eventually brought to see this by local rancher Tad Knight.

The circumstances of the family and their life in Clare are borne out by historical research and specific records and documentation. These included birth, marriage and death certificates, old newspaper texts, Griffiths Valuation Records, censuses – which for example revealed the existence, and age, of their servant Annie – and transcripts of the Bessborough Commission to which Tom had been called as a witness. The character descriptions of Tom and Ellen were suggested by both of their obituaries in the *Clare Journal*. Ellen's spoke of her as a woman of kindly and charitable disposition, and Tom was described as having had "the esteem and confidence of all classes because of his sterling probity".

The land legislation introduced at this time provided security of tenure and fair rents for tenant farmers and the right to compensation for any improvements made. The face of rural Ireland was changing dramatically in the wake of the Famine and mass emigration, the changes driven by agrarian upheaval and the activities of the Land League and the Irish Parliamentary Party. There was a shift from tillage to pasturage much lamented by agricultural advisors of the day. The influence of the temperance movement was widespread and active in founding and running sports activities for young people.

I supplemented my reading with research on the internet. Particularly helpful was the excellent Clare Library web site, with its wealth of information on local history. The Battle of Bodyke was vividly described here charting the involvement of the local farmers and priests. It was here also that I found evidence of the existence of Reading School in Quin, and discovered that cricket was the most popular sport in St Flannan's college at that time. I found a wonderfully informative site on the Casper Irish, and on the history of the Catholic Church in Wyoming, including the parish of Casper.

Both my mother and uncle were clear that Louis had been the first choice to go to Clare, and that he had been unable to settle. They also spoke of him remaining to settle Vincent in, before returning to Wyoming. Family lore told of Vincent returning to Wyoming a number of times to visit the family. The choice of 1891 as the likely date of his first visit was based on a belief that this would have given him enough time to settle into life in Clare and consolidate his attachments there, which could have been undermined by too premature a visit. We know from my Uncle Jack that his father once volunteered to ride rodeo when they visited a circus and won five pounds for doing so. He must have acquired this skill on his visits to Wyoming.

Records confirm that John Jo had been a Justice of the Peace from January 1891 through to June 1892, and that he died in Denver Hospital at the age of fifty-four of cancer of the liver. There are also records showing that Kate, Jack and Louis all applied for naturalisation and were granted citizenship, and that Kate successfully applied for irrigation rights before entering the priory.

A J Mokler, in his *History of Natrona County*, devotes a section to an account of the murder and robbery of Jack in 1920. He states that while the ranch was ransacked for money, hundreds of pounds worth of jewellery was left untouched. This was worth a lot of money then, and must have been rare enough to find in the homesteads of the west.

My mother spoke of Kate having written to Tom, when Vincent was about sixteen, to ask that legal arrangements be made to secure his future, indicating that if this was not done, she would have to bring him back to Wyoming as this had been the understanding upon which he had been sent to Clare. It was also my mother who told me that Kate wrote to him faithfully once a month, and used to send books over regularly. When she entered the priory he used to visit once a year, but could only see her through the small wire grill inserted into the wall, through which they spoke.

Chapter 11

There is substantial documentation confirming Kate's entry and death in Holy Cross Priory, Stapehill in Dorset ; i.e. certificate of profession, her own "last will and testament", a letter from Sister Veronica to my grandfather after Kate's death, and her death certificate. Though I read reasonably widely about religious life, I found two sources particularly useful in conveying a sense of the reality of Kate's life there: *La Trappe in England*, the work of an unknown religious writer, chronicling the history and growth of the Cistercian Order and of Holy Cross Priory itself, as well as the way of life espoused by Cistercians; and the writings of the Trappist monk Thomas Merton.

I strove to stay true to what was known of the story within the family, unless newly uncovered records indicated otherwise; e.g. Kate's decision to give up music as a sacrifice, or Pat's death at the age of thirty just before he was due to go on stage in New York, and John Jo's reputed fondness for drink. Indeed, as regards this last, his death at just fifty-four of cancer of the liver would suggest that it had substance. There are two slightly different versions of Pat's death and stage career within family lore, the one states that he died on stage and that he was an operatic singer, the other, that he died just before going on stage and that he was an actor and musician. I opted for the latter thinking it more likely in the circumstances of his life. The many gaps in the story are plugged by imagination, and the characterisation, dialogue and minor characters introduced to build up the story are all fictional. I did however, try to embed it in real historical circumstances, and interweave the characters' lives with real events.

Lightning Source UK Ltd.
Milton Keynes UK
20 November 2009

146513UK00001B/167/P